Bilingual
VISUAL
dictionary

Bilingual VISUAL dictionary

A DORLING KINDERSLEY BOOK

London, New York, Melbourne, Munich, Delhi

Senior Editor Angeles Gavira
Senior Art Editor Ina Stradins
DTP Designers Sunil Sharma, Balwant Singh,
Harish Aggarwal, John Goldsmid, Ashwani Tyagi
DTP Coordinator Pankaj Sharma
Production Controller Liz Cherry
Picture Researcher Anna Grapes
Managing Editor Liz Wheeler
Managing Art Editor Phil Ormerod
Category Publisher Jonathan Metcalf

Designed for Dorling Kindersley by WaltonCreative.com
Art Editor Colin Walton, assisted by Tracy Musson
Designers Peter Radcliffe, Earl Neish, Ann Cannings
Picture Research Marissa Keating

Language content for Dorling Kindersley by
g-and-w PUBLISHING
Managed by Jane Wightwick, assisted by Ana Bremón
Translation and editing by Christine Arthur
Additional input by Dr. Arturo Pretel, Martin Prill,
Frédéric Monteil, Meinrad Prill, Mari Bremón,
Oscar Bremón, Anunchi Bremón, Leila Gaafar

First published in Great Britain in 2005
by Dorling Kindersley Limited,
80 Strand, London WC2R 0RL
Copyright © 2005 Dorling Kindersley Limited
A Penguin Company

Content first published as
5 Language Visual Dictionary in 2003
Copyright © 2005 Dorling Kindersley Limited, London

ISBN-13: 978 4053 1120 5
ISBN-10: 1 4053 1120 7

Colour reproduction by Colourscan, Singapore
Printed and bound by L Rex

See our complete catalogue at
www.dk.com

table des matières
contents

TABLE DES MATIÈRES • CONTENTS

sortir manger •
eating out

l'étude • study

le travail • work

le transport •
transport

les sports • sport

le temps libre •
leisure

l'environnement •
environment

l'information •
reference

à propos du dictionnaire

Il est bien connu que les illustrations nous aident à comprendre et retenir l'information. Fondé sur ce principe, ce dictionnaire bilingue richement illustré présente un large éventail de vocabulaire courant et utile dans deux langues européennes.

Le dictionnaire est divisé de façon thématique et couvre en détail la plupart des aspects du monde quotidien, du restaurant au gymnase, de la maison au lieu de travail, de l'espace au monde animal. Vous y trouverez également des mots et expressions supplémentaires pour la conversation et pour enrichir votre vocabulaire.

Il s'agit d'un outil de référence essentiel pour tous ceux qui s'intéressent aux langues – pratique, stimulant et d'emploi facile.

Quelques points à noter

Les deux langues sont toujours présentées dans le même ordre – français et anglais.

Les noms sont donnés avec leurs articles définis qui indiquent leur genre (masculin ou féminin) et leur nombre (singulier ou pluriel):

| **la graine** | **les amendes** |
| seed | almonds |

Les verbes sont indiqués par un (v), par exemple:

récolter • harvest (v)

Chaque langue a également son propre index à la fin du livre. Vous pourrez y vérifier un mot dans n'importe laquelle des deux langues et vous serez renvoyé au(x) numéro(s) de(s) page(s) où il figure. Le genre est indiqué par les abréviations suivantes:

m = masculin
f = féminin

about the dictionary

The use of pictures is proven to aid understanding and the retention of information. Working on this principle, this highly-illustrated bilingual dictionary presents a large range of useful current vocabulary in two European languages.

The dictionary is divided thematically and covers most aspects of the everyday world in detail, from the restaurant to the gym, the home to the workplace, outer space to the animal kingdom. You will also find additional words and phrases for conversational use and for extending your vocabulary.

This is an essential reference tool for anyone interested in languages – practical, stimulating, and easy-to-use.

A few things to note

The two languages are always presented in the same order – French and English.

Nouns are given with their definite articles reflecting the gender (masculine or feminine) and number (singular or plural), for example:

| **la graine** | **les amendes** |
| seed | almonds |

Verbs are indicated by a (v) after the English, for example:

récolter • harvest (v)

Each language also has its own index at the back of the book. Here you can look up a word in either of the two languages and be referred to the page number(s) where it appears. The gender is shown using the following abbreviations:

m = masculine
f = feminine

comment utiliser ce livre

how to use this book

Que vous appreniez une nouvelle langue pour les affaires, le plaisir ou pour préparer vos vacances, ou encore si vous espérez élargir votre vocabulaire dans une langue qui vous est déjà familière, ce dictionnaire sera pour vous un outil d'apprentissage précieux que vous pourrez utiliser de plusieurs manières.

Lorsque vous apprenez une nouvelle langue, recherchez les mots apparentés (mots qui se ressemblent dans différentes langues) et les faux amis (mots qui se ressemblent mais ont des significations nettement différentes). Par exemple, l'anglais a importé des autres langues européennes de nombreux termes désignant la nourriture mais, en retour, exporté des termes employés dans le domaine de la technologie et de la culture populaire.

Whether you are learning a new language for business, pleasure, or in preparation for a holiday abroad, or are hoping to extend your vocabulary in an already familiar language, this dictionary is a valuable learning tool which you can use in a number of different ways.

When learning a new language, look out for cognates (words that are alike in different languages) and false friends (words that look alike but carry significantly different meanings). You can also see where the languages have influenced each other. For example, English has imported many terms for food from other European languages but, in turn, exported terms used in technology and popular culture.

Activités pratiques d'apprentissage

• Lorsque vous vous déplacez dans votre maison, au travail ou à l'université, essayez de regarder les pages qui correspondent à ce contexte. Vous pouvez ensuite fermer le livre, regarder autour de vous et voir combien d'objets vous pouvez nommer.
• Forcez-vous à écrire une histoire, une lettre ou un dialogue en employant le plus de termes possibles choisis dans une page. Ceci vous aidera à retenir le vocabulaire et son orthographe. Si vous souhaitez pouvoir écrire un texte plus long, commencez par des phrases qui incorporent 2 à 3 mots.
• Si vous avez une mémoire très visuelle, essayez de dessiner ou de décalquer des objets du livre sur une feuille de papier, puis fermez le livre et inscrivez les mots sous l'image.
• Une fois que vous serez plus sûr de vous, choisissez des mots dans l'index de la langue étrangère et essayez de voir si vous en connaissez le sens avant de vous reporter à la page correspondante pour vérifier.

Practical learning activities

• As you move about your home, workplace, or college, try looking at the pages which cover that setting. You could then close the book, look around you and see how many of the objects and features you can name.
• Challenge yourself to write a story, letter, or dialogue using as many of the terms on a particular page as possible. This will help you retain the vocabulary and remember the spelling. If you want to build up to writing a longer text, start with sentences incorporating 2–3 words.
• If you have a very visual memory, try drawing or tracing items from the book onto a piece of paper, then close the book and fill in the words below the picture.
• Once you are more confident, pick out words in a foreign-language index and see if you know what they mean before turning to the relevant page to check if you were right.

les gens
people

le corps • body

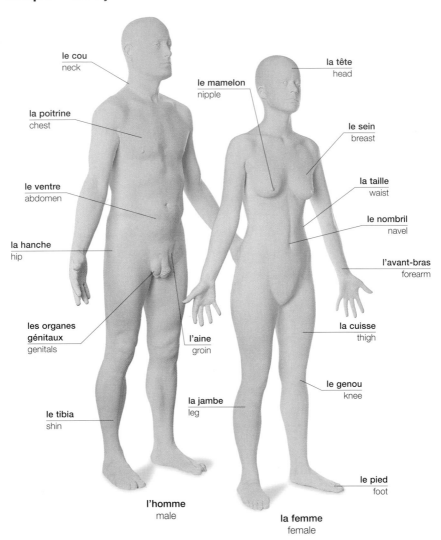

le cou
neck

la tête
head

le mamelon
nipple

la poitrine
chest

le sein
breast

la taille
waist

le ventre
abdomen

le nombril
navel

la hanche
hip

l'avant-bras
forearm

les organes
génitaux
genitals

l'aine
groin

la cuisse
thigh

le genou
knee

le tibia
shin

la jambe
leg

le pied
foot

l'homme
male

la femme
female

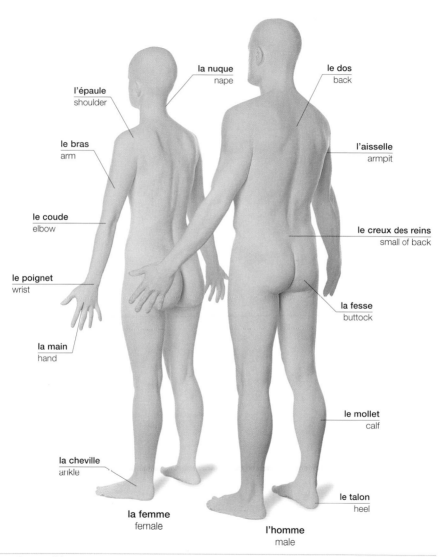

la nuque
nape

le dos
back

l'épaule
shoulder

le bras
arm

l'aisselle
armpit

le coude
elbow

le creux des reins
small of back

le poignet
wrist

la fesse
buttock

la main
hand

le mollet
calf

la cheville
ankle

le talon
heel

la femme
female

l'homme
male

le visage • face

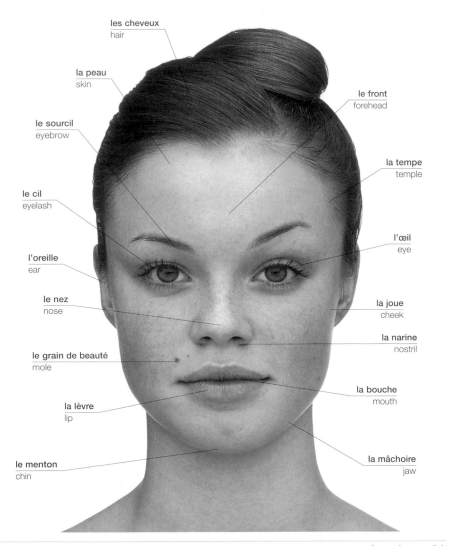

les cheveux
hair

la peau
skin

le front
forehead

le sourcil
eyebrow

la tempe
temple

le cil
eyelash

l'œil
eye

l'oreille
ear

le nez
nose

la joue
cheek

la narine
nostril

le grain de beauté
mole

la bouche
mouth

la lèvre
lip

la lèvre
lip

le menton
chin

la mâchoire
jaw

la ride
wrinkle

la tache de rousseur
freckle

le pore
pore

la fossette
dimple

la main • hand

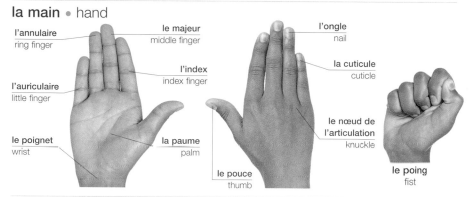

l'annulaire
ring finger

le majeur
middle finger

l'ongle
nail

l'index
index finger

la cuticule
cuticle

l'auriculaire
little finger

le poignet
wrist

la paume
palm

le nœud de l'articulation
knuckle

le pouce
thumb

le poing
fist

le pied • foot

le gros orteil
big toe

l'ongle du pied
toenail

l'avant-pied
ball

l'orteil
toe

le talon
heel

le petit orteil
little toe

le dos du pied
bridge

la plante du pied
sole

le cou-de-pied
instep

la cambrure
arch

la cheville
ankle

les muscles • muscles

le frontal
frontal

l'intercostal
intercostal

le biceps
biceps

les abdominaux
abdominals

les quadriceps
quadriceps

le pectoral
pectoral

le deltoïde
deltoid

le tendon
du jarret
hamstring

le tendon
d'Achille
Achilles tendon

le trapèze
trapezius

le dorsal
latissimus dorsi

le triceps
triceps

le fessier
buttock

les muscles
jumeaux
calf

le squelette • skeleton

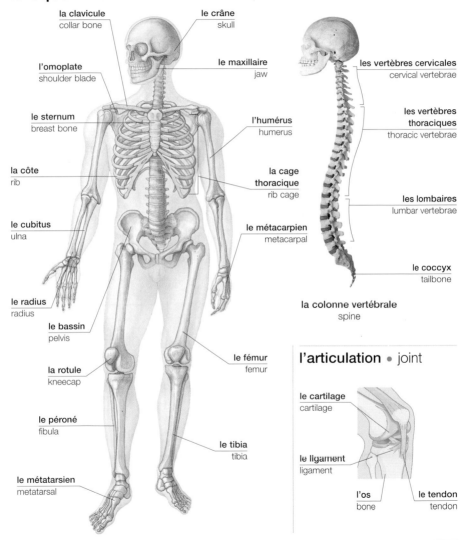

la clavicule
collar bone

le crâne
skull

l'omoplate
shoulder blade

le maxillaire
jaw

le sternum
breast bone

l'humérus
humerus

la côte
rib

la cage
thoracique
rib cage

le cubitus
ulna

le métacarpien
metacarpal

le radius
radius

le bassin
pelvis

la rotule
kneecap

le fémur
femur

le péroné
fibula

le tibia
tibia

le métatarsien
metatarsal

les vertèbres cervicales
cervical vertebrae

les vertèbres
thoraciques
thoracic vertebrae

les lombaires
lumbar vertebrae

le coccyx
tailbone

la colonne vertébrale
spine

l'articulation • joint

le cartilage
cartilage

le ligament
ligament

l'os
bone

le tendon
tendon

les organes internes • internal organs

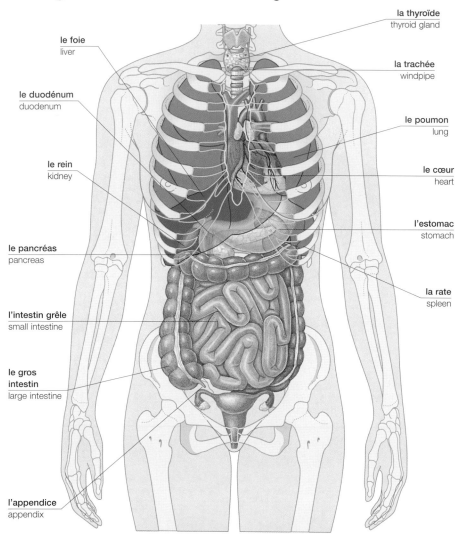

la thyroïde
thyroid gland

le foie
liver

la trachée
windpipe

le duodénum
duodenum

le poumon
lung

le rein
kidney

le cœur
heart

l'estomac
stomach

le pancréas
pancreas

la rate
spleen

l'intestin grêle
small intestine

le gros
intestin
large intestine

l'appendice
appendix

la tête • head

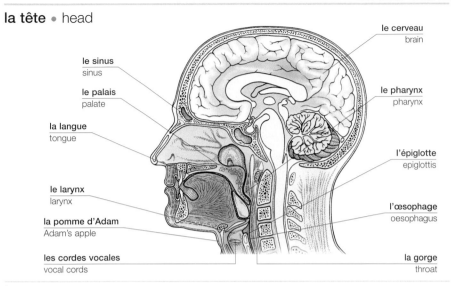

le cerveau
brain

le sinus
sinus

le palais
palate

la langue
tongue

le pharynx
pharynx

l'épiglotte
epiglottis

le larynx
larynx

l'œsophage
oesophagus

la pomme d'Adam
Adam's apple

les cordes vocales
vocal cords

la gorge
throat

les systèmes du corps • body systems

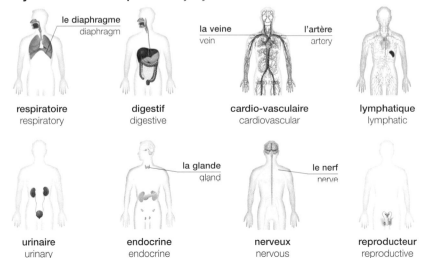

le diaphragme
diaphragm

la veine
vein

l'artère
artery

respiratoire
respiratory

digestif
digestive

cardio-vasculaire
cardiovascular

lymphatique
lymphatic

la glande
gland

le nerf
nerve

urinaire
urinary

endocrine
endocrine

nerveux
nervous

reproducteur
reproductive

les organes de reproduction • reproductive organs

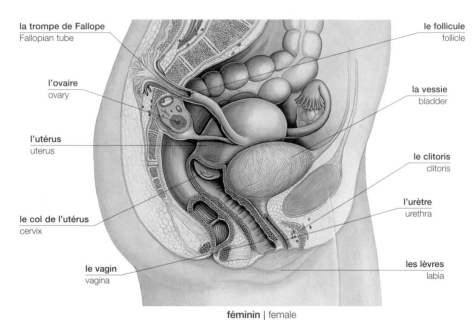

la trompe de Fallope Fallopian tube	le follicule follicle
l'ovaire ovary	la vessie bladder
l'utérus uterus	le clitoris clitoris
le col de l'utérus cervix	l'urètre urethra
le vagin vagina	les lèvres labia

féminin | female

la reproduction • reproduction

le sperme
sperm

l'ovule
egg

la fertilisation | fertilization

vocabulaire • vocabulary

l'hormone hormone	**impuissant** impotent	**les règles** menstruation
l'ovulation ovulation	**fécond** fertile	**les rapports sexuels** intercourse
stérile infertile	**concevoir** conceive	**la maladie sexuellement transmissible** sexually transmitted disease

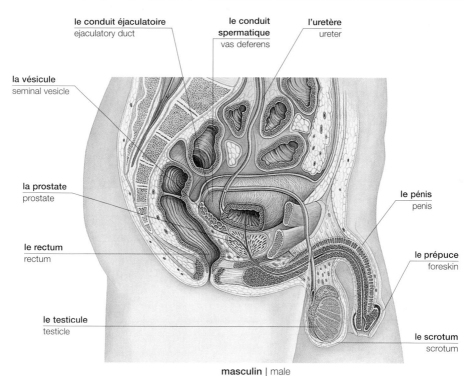

le conduit éjaculatoire
ejaculatory duct

le conduit
spermatique
vas deferens

l'uretère
ureter

la vésicule
seminal vesicle

la prostate
prostate

le pénis
penis

le rectum
rectum

le prépuce
foreskin

le testicule
testicle

le scrotum
scrotum

masculin | male

la contraception • contraception

**la cape
cervicale**
cap

le diaphragme
diaphragm

le condom
condom

le stérilet
IUD

la pilule
pill

la famille • family

la grand-mère
grandmother

le grand-père
grandfather

l'oncle
uncle

la tante
aunt

le père
father

la mère
mother

le cousin
cousin

le frère
brother

la sœur
sister

la femme
wife

la belle-fille
daughter-in-law

le fils
son

la fille
daughter

le gendre
son-in-law

le petit-fils
grandson

la petite-fille
granddaughter

le mari
husband

vocabulaire • vocabulary

les parents relatives	**les parents** parents	**les petits-enfants** grandchildren	**la belle-mère** stepmother	**le beau-fils** stepson	**la génération** generation
les grands-parents grandparents	**les enfants** children	**le beau-père** stepfather	**la belle-fille** stepdaughter	**le/la partenaire** partner	**les jumeaux** twins

la belle-mère
mother-in-law

le beau-père
father-in-law

le beau-frère
brother-in-law

la belle-sœur
sister-in-law

la nièce
niece

le neveu
nephew

les titres • titles

Madame
Mrs

Monsieur
Mr

Mademoiselle
Miss

les stades • stages

le bébé
baby

l'enfant
child

le garçon
boy

la fille
girl

l'adolescente
teenager

l'adulte
adult

l'homme
man

la femme
woman

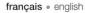

les relations • relationships

le chef
manager

l'assistante
assistant

l'associée
business partner

l'employeuse
employer

l'employé
employee

le collègue
colleague

le bureau | office

le voisin
neighbour

l'ami
friend

la connaissance
acquaintance

le correspondant
penfriend

le petit ami
boyfriend

la petite amie
girlfriend

le couple | couple

le fiancé
fiancé

la fiancée
fiancée

les fiancés | engaged couple

les émotions • emotions

le sourire
smile

heureux
happy

triste
sad

excité
excited

ennuyé
bored

surpris
surprised

effrayé
scared

le froncement
de sourcils
frown

fâché
angry

confus
confused

inquiet
worried

nerveux
nervous

fier
proud

confiant
confident

gêné
embarrassed

timide
shy

vocabulaire • vocabulary

consterné	rire	**soupirer**	crier
upset	laugh (v)	sigh (v)	shout (v)
choqué	pleurer	**s'évanouir**	bâiller
shocked	cry (v)	faint (v)	yawn (v)

les événements de la vie • life events

naître
be born (v)

commencer à l'école
start school (v)

se faire des amis
make friends (v)

obtenir sa licence
graduate (v)

trouver un emploi
get a job (v)

tomber amoureux
fall in love (v)

se marier
get married (v)

avoir un bébé
have a baby (v)

le mariage | wedding

le divorce
divorce

l'enterrement
funeral

vocabulaire • vocabulary

le baptême christening	**mourir** die (v)
la bar-mitsvah bar mitzvah	**faire son testament** make a will (v)
l'anniversaire de mariage anniversary	**l'acte de naissance** birth certificate
émigrer emigrate (v)	**le repas de noces** wedding reception
prendre sa retraite retire (v)	**le voyage de noces** honeymoon

les fêtes • celebrations

la fête
birthday party

la carte
card

le cadeau
present

l'anniversaire
birthday

le Noël
Christmas

les fêtes •
festivals

la Pâque
Passover

le Nouvel An
New Year

le carnaval
carnival

le défilé
procession

le Ramadan
Ramadan

le ruban
ribbon

la fête de Thanksgiving
Thanksgiving

Pâques
Easter

la veille de la Toussaint
Halloween

la Diwali
Diwali

l'apparence
appearance

les vêtements d'enfants • children's clothing

le bébé • baby

la combinaison de neige
snowsuit

le tricot de corps
vest

le bouton-pression
popper

la grenouillère
babygro

le pyjama
sleepsuit

la combinaison-short
romper suit

le bavoir
bib

les moufles
mittens

les chaussons
booties

la couche éponge
terry nappy

la couche jetable
disposable nappy

la culotte en plastique
plastic pants

le petit enfant • toddler

le t-shirt
t-shirt

la salopette
dungarees

le chapeau de soleil
sunhat

le tablier
apron

le bermuda
shorts

la jupe
skirt

l'enfant • child

la robe
dress

la capuche
hood

le jean
jeans

le sac à dos
backpack

le bouton
toggle

l'écharpe
scarf

l'anorak
anorak

les sandales
sandals

les bottes de caoutchouc
wellington boots

l'été
summer

l'imperméable
raincoat

l'automne
autumn

le duffel-coat
duffel coat

l'hiver
winter

la robe de chambre
dressing gown

le logo
logo

les baskets
trainers

la chemise de nuit
nightie

les pantoufles
slippers

les vêtements de nuit
nightwear

la tenue de foot
football strip

le survêtement
tracksuit

les leggings
leggings

vocabulaire • vocabulary

la fibre naturelle natural fibre	**C'est lavable en machine?** Is it machine washable?
synthétique synthetic	**C'est la bonne taille pour deux ans?** Will this fit a two-year-old?

les vêtements pour hommes • men's clothing

le col
collar

la cravate
tie

la ceinture
belt

le revers
lapel

la boutonnière
buttonhole

la manchette
cuff

la poche
pocket

la veste
jacket

le pantalon
trousers

le bouton
button

les chaussures en cuir
leather shoes

la doublure
lining

le costume
business suit

le manteau
coat

vocabulaire • vocabulary

la chemise shirt	**le peignoir** dressing gown	**le survêtement** tracksuit	**long** long
le cardigan cardigan	**les sous-vêtements** underwear	**l'imperméable** raincoat	**court** short

Avez-vous ça en plus grand/petit?
Do you have this in a larger/smaller size?

Je peux l'essayer?
May I try this on?

le blazer
blazer

la veste de sport
sports jacket

le gilet
waistcoat

l'encolure en V
v-neck

le col rond
round neck

le t-shirt
t-shirt

l'anorak
anorak

le sweat-shirt
sweatshirt

le coupe-vent
windcheater

le pantalon de jogging
sweatpants

le pullover
sweater

le pyjama
pyjamas

le tricot de corps
vest

les vêtements sport
casual wear

le short
shorts

le slip
briefs

le caleçon
boxer shorts

les chaussettes
socks

les vêtements pour femmes • women's clothing

la veste
jacket

l'encolure
neckline

la couture
seam

la manche
sleeve

long
ankle length

la jupe
skirt

l'ourlet
hem

à genou
knee-length

les collants
tights

les chaussures
shoes

sans
bretelles
strapless

sans manches
sleeveless

la robe du soir
evening dress

la robe
dress

le chemisier
blouse

le pantalon
trousers

décontracté
casual

la lingerie • lingerie

le négligé
negligée

le caraco
slip

la bretelle
strap

la camisole
camisole

la jarretelle
suspenders

la guêpière
basque

les bas
stockings

le collant
tights

la chemise
vest

le soutien-gorge
bra

le slip
knickers

la chemise de nuit
nightdress

le mariage • wedding

la dentelle
lace

le voile
veil

le bouquet
bouquet

la traîne
train

la robe de mariée
wedding dress

vocabulaire • vocabulary

le corset corset	**ajusté** tailored
la jarretière garter	**dos-nu** halter neck
l'épaulette shoulder pad	**à armature** underwired
la ceinture waistband	**le soutien-gorge sport** sports bra

les accessoires • accessories

la casquette
cap

le chapeau
hat

le foulard
scarf

la ceinture
belt

la boucle
buckle

le manche
handle

la pointe
tip

le mouchoir
handkerchief

le nœud papillon
bow tie

l'épingle de cravate
tie-pin

les gants
gloves

le parapluie
umbrella

les bijoux • jewellery

le pendentif
pendant

la broche
brooch

le bouton de manchette
cufflink

le rang de perles
string of pearls

le maillon
link

le fermoir
clasp

la boucle d'oreille
earring

la bague
ring

la pierre
stone

le collier
necklace

la montre
watch

le bracelet
bracelet

la chaîne
chain

la boîte à bijoux | jewellery box

les sacs • bags

le portefeuille
wallet

le porte-monnaie
purse

le sac à bandoulière
shoulder bag

le fermoir
fastening

la bretelle
shoulder strap

les poignées
handles

le fourre-tout
holdall

la serviette
briefcase

le sac à main
handbag

le sac à dos
backpack

les chaussures • shoes

l'œillet
eyelet

le lacet
lace

la languette
tongue

la semelle
sole

le talon
heel

la chaussure lacée
lace-up

le pataugas
walking boot

la basket
trainer

la chaussure de cuir
leather shoe

la tong
flip-flop

la chaussure à talon
high heel shoe

la chaussure à semelle compensée
platform shoe

la sandale
sandal

le mocassin
slip-on

le richelieu
brogue

les cheveux • hair

le peigne
comb

peigner
comb (v)

la brosse
brush

brosser | brush (v)

la coiffeuse
hairdresser

le lavabo
sink

la cliente
client

laver | wash (v)

le peignoir
robe

rincer
rinse (v)

couper
cut (v)

sécher
blow dry (v)

faire une mise en plis
set (v)

---

les accessoires • accessories

le sèche-cheveux
hairdryer

le shampoing
shampoo

l'après-shampoing
conditioner

le gel
gel

la laque
hairspray

le fer à friser
curling tongs

les ciseaux
scissors

le serre-tête
hairband

le bigoudi
curler

la pince à cheveux
hairpin

les coiffures • styles

le ruban
ribbon

la queue de cheval
ponytail

la natte
plait

le rouleau
french pleat

le chignon
bun

les couettes
pigtails

au carré
bob

la coupe courte
crop

frisé
curly

la permanente
perm

raide
straight

les racines
roots

les reflets
highlights

chauve
bald

la perruque
wig

les couleurs • colours

blond
blonde

châtain
brunette

auburn
auburn

roux
ginger

noir
black

gris
grey

blanc
white

teint
dyed

la beauté • beauty

la teinture de cheveux
hair dye

le fard à paupières
eye shadow

le mascara
mascara

l'eye-liner
eyeliner

le fard à joues
blusher

le fond de teint
foundation

le rouge à lèvres
lipstick

le maquillage • make-up

le crayon à sourcils
eyebrow pencil

la brosse à sourcils
eyebrow brush

la pince à épiler
tweezers

le brillant à lèvres
lip gloss

le pinceau à lèvres
lip brush

le crayon à lèvres
lip liner

le pinceau
brush

le correcteur
concealer

le miroir
mirror

la poudre
face powder

la houppette
powder puff

le poudrier | compact

les soins de beauté • beauty treatments

le masque
de beauté
face pack

le lit U.V.
sunbed

le soin du visage
facial

exfolier
exfoliate (v)

l'épilation
wax

la pédicurie
pedicure

la manucure • manicure

le dissolvant
nail varnish remover

la lime à ongles
nail file

le vernis à ongles
nail varnish

les ciseaux à
ongles
nail scissors

le coupe-
ongles
nail clippers

les accessoires de toilette • toiletries

le démaquillant
cleanser

le tonique
toner

la crème
hydratante
moisturizer

l'autobronzant
self-tanning cream

le parfum
perfume

l'eau de toilette
eau de toilette

vocabulaire • vocabulary

le teint complexion	gras oily	le bronzage tan
clair fair	sensible sensitive	le tatouage tattoo
foncé dark	hypoallergénique hypoallergenic	antirides anti-wrinkle
sec dry	le ton shade	les boules de coton cotton balls

la santé
health

la maladie • illness

la fièvre | fever

le mal de tête
headache

le saignement de nez
nosebleed

la toux
cough

l'éternuement
sneeze

le rhume
cold

la grippe
flu

l'inhalateur
inhaler

l'asthme
asthma

les crampes
cramps

la nausée
nausea

la varicelle
chickenpox

l'éruption
rash

---

vocabulaire • vocabulary

l'attaque stroke	**le diabète** diabetes	**l'eczéma** eczema	**le refroidissement** chill	**vomir** vomit (v)	**la diarrhée** diarrhoea
la tension blood pressure	**l'allergie** allergy	**l'infection** infection	**le mal d'estomac** stomach ache	**l'épilepsie** epilepsy	**la rougeole** measles
la crise cardiaque heart attack	**le rhume des foins** hayfever	**le virus** virus	**s'évanouir** faint (v)	**la migraine** migraine	**les oreillons** mumps

---

le médecin • doctor
la consultation • consultation

le médecin
doctor

la lampe de radio
x-ray viewer

l'ordonnance
prescription

la patiente
patient

la toise
height bar

l'infirmière
nurse

la balance
scales

le sphygmotensiomètre
blood pressure gauge

le stéthoscope
stethoscope

le manchon
cuff

vocabulaire • vocabulary

le rendez-vous appointment	l'inoculation inoculation
le cabinet surgery	le thermomètre thermometer
la salle d'attente waiting room	l'examen médical medical examination

J'ai besoin de voir un médecin.
I need to see a doctor.

J'ai mal ici.
It hurts here.

la blessure • injury

l'écharpe
sling

la minerve
neck brace

l'entorse | sprain

la fracture
fracture

le coup du lapin
whiplash

la coupure
cut

l'écorchure
graze

la contusion
bruise

l'écharde
splinter

le coup de soleil
sunburn

la brûlure
burn

la morsure
bite

la piqûre
sting

vocabulaire • vocabulary

l'accident accident	**l'hémorragie** haemorrhage	**l'empoisonnement** poisoning	**Est-ce qu'il/elle va se remettre?** Will he/she be all right?
l'urgence emergency	**l'ampoule** blister	**le choc électrique** electric shock	**Où avez-vous mal?** Where does it hurt?
la blessure wound	**la commotion cérébrale** concussion	**le traumatisme crânien** head injury	**Appelez une ambulance s'il vous plaît.** Please call an ambulance.

les premiers secours • first aid

la pommade
ointment

le pansement
plaster

l'épingle de
sûreté
safety pin

le bandage
bandage

les analgésiques
painkillers

la serviette
antiseptique
antiseptic wipe

la pince fine
tweezers

les ciseaux
scissors

l'antiseptique
antiseptic

la trousse de premiers secours | first aid box

la gaze
gauze

le pansement
dressing

l'attelle | splint

le sparadrap
adhesive tape

la réanimation
resuscitation

vocabulaire • vocabulary			
le choc shock	le pouls pulse	étouffer choke (v)	**Est-ce que vous pouvez m'aider?** Can you help?
sans connaissance unconscious	la respiration breathing	stérile sterile	**Pouvez-vous donner les soins d'urgence?** Do you know first aid?

l'hôpital • hospital

le chirurgien
surgeon

la courbe
chart

l'anesthésiste
anaesthetist

l'infirmière
nurse

la salle d'opération
operating theatre

l'analyse de sang
blood test

l'injection
injection

la radio
x-ray

la scanographie
scan

le chariot
trolley

le bouton d'appel
call button

la salle des urgences
emergency room

la salle
ward

la chaise roulante
wheelchair

---

vocabulaire • vocabulary

l'opération operation	**renvoyé** discharged	**les heures de visite** visiting hours	**la pédiatrie** children's ward	**le service de soins intensifs** intensive care unit
admis admitted	**la clinique** clinic	**la maternité** maternity ward	**la chambre privée** private room	**le malade en consultation externe** outpatient

---

les services • departments

l'O.R.L.
ENT

la cardiologie
cardiology

l'orthopédie
orthopaedy

la gynécologie
gynaecology

la kinésithérapie
physiotherapy

la dermatologie
dermatology

la pédiatrie
paediatrics

la radiologie
radiology

la chirurgie
surgery

la maternité
maternity

la psychiatrie
psychiatry

l'ophtalmologie
ophthalmology

---

vocabulaire • vocabulary

la neurologie neurology	**l'urologie** urology	**l'endocrinologie** endocrinology	**la pathologie** pathology	**le résultat** result
l'oncologie oncology	**la chirurgie esthétique** plastic surgery	**l'orientation d'un patient** referral	**l'analyse** test	**le spécialiste** consultant

---

le dentiste • dentist

la dent • tooth

l'émail
enamel

la gencive
gum

le nerf
nerve

la racine
root

la prémolaire
premolar

l'incisive
incisor

la molaire
molar

la canine
canine

la visite de contrôle • check-up

la lampe
reflector

la sonde
probe

le bavoir
apron

le crachoir
basin

le fauteuil de dentiste
dentist's chair

vocabulaire • vocabulary

la rage de dents toothache	**la fraise** drill
la plaque plaque	**le fil dentaire** dental floss
la carie decay	**l'extraction** extraction
le plombage filling	**la couronne** crown

utiliser le fil
dentaire
floss (v)

brosser
brush

l'appareil
dentaire
brace

la radio dentaire
dental x-ray

la radio
x-ray film

le dentier
dentures

l'opticien • optician

l'étui
case

le verre
lens

la monture
frame

les lunettes
glasses

les lunettes de soleil
sunglasses

la solution nettoyante
cleaning fluid

la solution
désinfectante
disinfectant solution

l'étui à lentilles
lens case

l'examen de la vue | eye test

les lentilles de contact | contact lenses

l'œil • eye

le sourcil
eyebrow

la paupière
eyelid

la pupille
pupil

le cil
eyelash

l'iris
iris

la rétine
retina

le cristallin
lens

le nerf optique
optic nerve

la cornée
cornea

vocabulaire • vocabulary	
la vue vision	l'astigmatisme astigmatism
la dioptrie diopter	la presbytie long sight
la larme tear	la myopie short sight
la cataracte cataract	bifocal bifocal

la grossesse • pregnancy

l'infirmière
nurse

le test de grossesse
pregnancy test

l'échographie
scan

le cordon
ombilical
umbilical cord

le placenta
placenta

le col de l'utérus
cervix

l'utérus
uterus

les ultrasons | ultrasound

le fœtus | foetus

vocabulaire • vocabulary					
l'ovulation ovulation	**prénatal** antenatal	**l'amniocentèse** amniocentesis	**la dilatation** dilation	**l'accouchement** delivery	**par le siège** breech
la conception conception	**l'embryon** embryo	**la contraction** contraction	**la péridurale** epidural	**la naissance** birth	**prématuré** premature
enceinte pregnant	**l'utérus** womb	**perdre les eaux** break waters (v)	**l'épisiotomie** episiotomy	**la fausse couche** miscarriage	**le gynécologue** gynaecologist
enceinte expectant	**le trimestre** trimester	**le liquide amniotique** amniotic fluid	**la césarienne** caesarean section	**les points de suture** stitches	**l'obstétricien** obstetrician

la naissance • childbirth

la perfusion
drip

la sage-femme
midwife

le moniteur
monitor

le cathéter
catheter

déclencher l'accouchement
induce labour (v)

la couveuse | incubator

le pèse-bébé
scales

le poids de naissance | birth weight

le forceps
forceps

la ventouse
ventouse cup

l'accouchement assisté
assisted delivery

le bracelet d'identité
identity tag

le nouveau-né
newborn baby

l'allaitement • nursing

la pompe à lait
breast pump

**le soutien-gorge
d'allaitement**
nursing bra

donner le sein
breastfeed (v)

les coussinets
pads

les thérapies alternatives • alternative therapy

le maître
teacher

le massage
massage

le shiatsu
shiatsu

le yoga | yoga

le tapis
mat

la méditation
meditation

la chiropractie
chiropractic

l'ostéopathie
osteopathy

la réflexologie
reflexology

le conseiller
counsellor

le reiki
reiki

l'acuponcture
acupuncture

la thérapie de groupe
group therapy

la médecine ayurvédique
ayurveda

l'hypnothérapie
hypnotherapy

les huiles essentielles
essential oils

l'herboristerie
herbalism

l'aromathérapie
aromatherapy

l'homéopathie
homeopathy

l'acupression
acupressure

la thérapeute
therapist

la psychothérapie
psychotherapy

vocabulaire • vocabulary

le supplément supplement	**la naturopathie** naturopathy	**la relaxation** relaxation	**l'herbe** herb
l'hydrothérapie hydrotherapy	**le feng shui** feng shui	**le stress** stress	**la guérison** **par cristaux** crystal healing

la maison
home

la maison • house

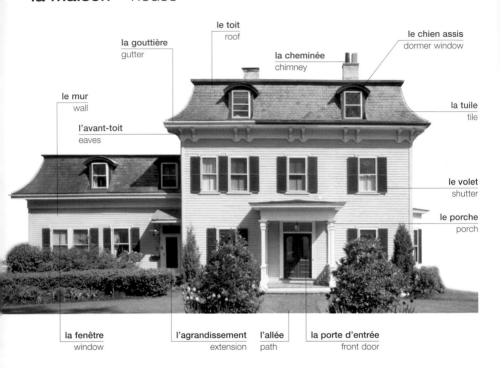

le toit
roof

la gouttière
gutter

la cheminée
chimney

le chien assis
dormer window

le mur
wall

la tuile
tile

l'avant-toit
eaves

le volet
shutter

le porche
porch

la fenêtre
window

l'agrandissement
extension

l'allée
path

la porte d'entrée
front door

vocabulaire • vocabulary

individuelle detached	le locataire tenant	le garage garage	la boîte aux lettres letterbox	l'alarme burglar alarm	louer rent (v)
mitoyenne semidetached	la pavillon bungalow	le grenier attic	la lampe d'entrée porch light	la cour courtyard	le loyer rent
la maison de deux étages townhouse	le sous-sol basement	la chambre room	le propriétaire landlord	l'étage floor	attenante terraced

l'entrée • entrance

la main
courante
hand rail

le palier
landing

la rampe
banister

l'escalier
staircase

le vestibule
hallway

la sonnette
doorbell

le paillasson
doormat

le marteau de porte
door knocker

la chaîne de sûreté
door chain

la clef
key

la serrure
lock

le verrou
bolt

l'appartement •
flat

le balcon
balcony

l'immeuble
block of flats

l'interphone
intercom

l'ascenseur
lift

les systèmes domestiques • internal systems

le radiateur
radiator

l'aile
blade

le ventilateur
fan

l'appareil de chauffage
heater

le convecteur
convector heater

l'électricité • electricity

le filament
filament

la mise à la terre
earthing

le culot à baïonnette
bayonet fitting

l'ampoule
light bulb

la broche
pin

la prise
plug

neutre
neutral

sous tension
live

les fils
wires

---

vocabulaire • vocabulary

la tension voltage	**le fusible** fuse	**la prise de courant** socket	**le courant continu** direct current	**la coupure de courant** power cut
l'ampère amp	**la boîte à fusibles** fuse box	**l'interrupteur** switch	**le transformateur** transformer	**le réseau d'électricité** mains supply
le courant power	**la génératrice** generator	**le courant alternatif** alternating current	**le compteur d'électricité** electricity meter	

---

la plomberie • plumbing

l'arrivée
inlet

la sortie
outlet

la soupape
de sûreté
pressure valve

l'isolation
insulation

le trop-plein
overflow pipe

le réservoir
tank

la chambre d'eau
water chamber

le robinet de purge
drain cock

le thermostat
thermostat

le brûleur à gaz
gas burner

la résistance
heating element

la chaudière
boiler

l'évier • sink

le robinet
tap

la manette
lever

le joint
gasket

la conduite d'amenée
supply pipe

le robinet de sectionnement
shutoff valve

le tuyau d'écoulement
drain

le broyeur d'ordures
waste disposal unit

les W.-C. • water closet

la chasse-d'eau
cistern

le flotteur
float ball

le siège
seat

la cuvette
bowl

le tuyau d'écoulement
waste pipe

l'enlèvement de déchets • waste disposal

la bouteille
bottle

le couvercle
lid

la pédale
pedal

la boîte à déchets recyclables
recycling bin

la poubelle
rubbish bin

la boîte de tri
sorting unit

les déchets bios
organic waste

le salon • living room

le tableau
painting

le cadre
frame

la lampe
lamp

l'applique
wall light

la pendule
clock

le plafond
ceiling

la vitrine
cabinet

le canapé
sofa

le coussin
cushion

la table
basse
coffee table

le sol
floor

le miroir
mirror

le vase
vase

la tablette de
cheminée
mantelpiece

la cheminée
fireplace

le garde-feu
screen

la bougie
candle

la bibliothèque
bookshelf

le canapé-lit
sofabed

le tapis
rug

le rideau
curtain

le brise-bise
net curtain

le store vénitien
venetian blind

le store
roller blind

la moulure
moulding

le fauteuil
armchair

le bureau | study

la salle à manger • dining room

le poivre
pepper

le sel
salt

la table
table

la vaisselle
crockery

les couverts
cutlery

la chaise
chair

le dossier
back

le siège
seat

le pied
leg

vocabulaire • vocabulary

mettre la table lay the table (v)	**(avoir) faim** hungry	**le déjeuner** lunch	**rassasié** full	**l'hôte** host
servir serve (v)	**la nappe** tablecloth	**le dîner** dinner	**la portion** portion	**l'hôtesse** hostess
manger eat (v)	**le petit déjeuner** breakfast	**le set de table** place mat	**le repas** meal	**l'invité** guest

Puis-je en reprendre un peu, s'il vous plaît?
Can I have some more, please?

Non merci, j'en ai eu assez.
I've had enough, thank you.

C'était délicieux.
That was delicious.

la vaisselle et les couverts • crockery and cutlery

la grande tasse
mug

la tasse à café
coffee cup

la cuiller à café
teaspoon

la tasse à thé
teacup

l'assiette
plate

le bol
bowl

la cafetière
cafetière

la théière
teapot

le pot
jug

le coquetier
egg cup

le verre à vin
wine glass

le verre
tumbler

la verrerie
glassware

le rond de
serviette
napkin ring

l'assiette à
dessert
side plate

l'assiette
plate
dinner plate

l'assiette à
soupe
soup bowl

la cuiller à soupe
soup spoon

la fourchette
fork

la serviette
napkin

le couvert
place setting

la cuiller
spoon

le couteau
knife

la cuisine • kitchen

l'étagère
shelves

le revêtement
splashback

le robinet
tap

l'évier
sink

le tiroir
drawer

la hotte
extractor

la table de
cuisson
céramique
ceramic hob

le plan de
travail
worktop

le four
oven

le placard
cabinet

les appareils ménagers • appliances

le micro-ondes
microwave oven

le bol du mixeur
mixing bowl

la lame
blade

le couvercle
lid

**la bouilloire
électrique**
kettle

le grille-pain
toaster

le robot ménager
food processor

le mixeur
blender

le lave-vaisselle
dishwasher

le freezer
ice maker

le
réfrigérateur
refrigerator

la clayette
shelf

le
congélateur
freezer

le bac à
légumes
crisper

le réfrigérateur-congélateur | fridge-freezer

vocabulaire • vocabulary	
l'égouttoir draining board	**congeler** freeze (v)
le brûleur burner	**décongeler** defrost (v)
la table de cuisson hob	**cuire à la vapeur** steam (v)
la poubelle rubbish bin	**faire sauter** sauté (v)

la cuisine • cooking

éplucher
peel (v)

couper
slice (v)

râper
grate (v)

verser
pour (v)

mélanger
mix (v)

battre
whisk (v)

bouillir
boil (v)

frire
fry (v)

étaler au rouleau
roll (v)

remuer
stir (v)

mijoter
simmer (v)

pocher
poach (v)

cuire au four
bake (v)

rôtir
roast (v)

griller
grill (v)

les ustensiles de cuisine • kitchenware

le couteau à pain
bread knife

la planche à hacher
chopping board

le couteau de cuisine
kitchen knife

le fendoir
cleaver

l'aiguisoir
knife sharpener

l'attendrisseur
meat tenderizer

la broche
skewer

le pilon
pestle

l'épluche-légume
peeler

le vide-pomme
apple corer

la râpe
grater

le mortier
mortar

le presse-purée
masher

l'ouvre-boîte
can opener

l'ouvre-bouteille
bottle opener

le presse-ail
garlic press

la cuiller à servir
serving spoon

la pelle à poisson
fish slice

la passoire
colander

la spatule
spatula

la cuiller en bois
wooden spoon

l'écumoire
slotted spoon

la louche
ladle

la fourchette à découper
carving fork

la cuiller à glace
scoop

le fouet
whisk

la passoire
sieve

le couvercle
lid

anti-adhérent
non-stick

la poêle
frying pan

la casserole
saucepan

le gril
grill pan

le wok
wok

le fait-tout
earthenware dish

en verre
glass

allant au four
ovenproof

le grand bol
mixing bowl

le moule à soufflé
soufflé dish

le plat à gratin
gratin dish

le ramequin
ramekin

la cocotte
casserole dish

la pâtisserie • baking cakes

la balance
scales

le verre mesureur
measuring jug

**le moule à
gâteaux**
cake tin

la tourtière
pie tin

le moule à tarte
flan tin

le pinceau à pâtisserie
pastry brush

le rouleau à pâtisserie
rolling pin

la poche à douille
piping bag

**le moule à
muffins**
muffin tray

**la plaque à
gâteaux**
baking tray

**la grille de
refroidissement**
cooling rack

le gant isolant
oven glove

le tablier
apron

la chambre • bedroom

l'armoire
wardrobe

la lampe de chevet
bedside lamp

la tête de lit
headboard

la table de nuit
bedside table

la commode
chest of drawers

le tiroir	le lit	le matelas	le couvre-lit	l'oreiller
drawer	bed	mattress	bedspread	pillow

la bouillotte
hot-water bottle

le radio-réveil
clock radio

le réveil
alarm clock

la boîte de kleenex
box of tissues

le cintre
coat hanger

le linge de lit • bed linen

le miroir
mirror

la coiffeuse
dressing
table

la taie d'oreiller
pillowcase

le drap
sheet

la frange de lit
valance

la couette
duvet

l'édredon
quilt

la
couverture
blanket

le sol
floor

vocabulaire • vocabulary

le lit simple single bed	**le pied de lit** footboard	**l'insomnie** insomnia	**se réveiller** wake up (v)	**mettre le réveil** set the alarm (v)
le grand lit double bed	**le ressort** spring	**se coucher** go to bed (v)	**se lever** get up (v)	**ronfler** snore (v)
la couverture chauffante electric blanket	**le tapis** carpet	**s'endormir** go to sleep (v)	**faire le lit** make the bed (v)	**l'armoire encastrée** built-in wardrobe

la salle de bain • bathroom

le porte-serviettes
towel rail

la porte de douche
shower door

le robinet d'eau froide
cold tap

le robinet d'eau chaude
hot tap

le pommeau de douche
shower head

le lavabo
washbasin

la bonde
plug

la douche
shower

le tuyau d'écoulement
drain

le siège des toilettes
toilet seat

les toilettes
toilet

la brosse
toilet brush

la baignoire
bathtub

le bidet | bidet

---

vocabulaire • vocabulary

l'armoire à pharmacie medicine cabinet	**le tapis de bain** bath mat
le rouleau de papier hygiénique toilet roll	**le rideau de douche** shower curtain
prendre une douche take a shower (v)	**prendre un bain** take a bath (v)

l'hygiène dentaire • dental hygiene

la brosse à dents
toothbrush

le dentifrice
toothpaste

le fil dentaire
dental floss

l'eau dentifrice
mouthwash

---

le luffa
loofah

l'éponge
sponge

la pierre ponce
pumice stone

la brosse pour le dos
back brush

le déodorant
deodorant

le porte-savon
soap dish

le savon
soap

le gel douche
shower gel

la crème pour le visage
face cream

le bain moussant
bubble bath

la serviette
hand towel

la serviette
de bain
bath towel

les serviettes
towels

la lotion pour le corps
body lotion

le talc
talcum powder

le peignoir
bathrobe

le rasage • shaving

le rasoir
électrique
electric razor

la mousse à raser
shaving foam

le rasoir jetable
disposable razor

la lame de
rasoir
razor blade

l'after-shave
aftershave

la chambre d'enfants • nursery

les soins de bébé • baby care

la crème pour l'érythème
nappy rash cream

l'éponge
sponge

la lingette
wet wipe

la baignoire en plastique
baby bath

le pot
potty

le matelas à langer
changing mat

le coucher • sleeping

le mobile
mobile

le drap
sheet

la couverture
blanket

les barreaux
bars

la couverture laineuse
fleece

la literie
bedding

le protège-barreaux
bumper

le matelas
mattress

le lit d'enfant | cot

le hochet
rattle

le moïse
moses basket

le jeu • playing

la poupée
doll

le jouet en peluche
soft toy

la maison de poupée
doll's house

la maison pliante
playhouse

la sécurité • safety

la serrure de
sécurité
child lock

le moniteur
baby monitor

l'ours en peluche
teddy bear

le jouet
toy

le panier à jouets
toy basket

la balle
ball

le parc
playpen

la barrière d'escalier
stair gate

le manger • eating

la chaise haute
high chair

la tétine
teat

la tasse
drinking cup

le biberon
bottle

la sortie • going out

la poussette
pushchair

la capote
hood

le landau
pram

le couffin
carrycot

la couche
nappy

le sac
changing bag

le porte-bébé
baby sling

la buanderie • utility room

le linge • laundry

le linge sale
dirty washing

le linge propre
clean clothes

le panier à linge
laundry basket

le lave-linge
washing machine

le lave-linge séchant
washer-dryer

le sèche-linge
tumble dryer

le panier à linge
linen basket

la corde à linge
clothes line

le fer à repasser
iron

la pince à linge
clothes peg

sécher
dry (v)

la planche à repasser | ironing board

---

vocabulaire • vocabulary

charger load (v)	**essorer** spin (v)	**repasser** iron (v)	**Comment fonctionne le lave-linge?** How do I operate the washing machine?
rincer rinse (v)	**l'essoreuse** spin dryer	**l'assouplisseur** conditioner	**Quel est le programme pour les couleurs/le blanc?** What is the setting for coloureds/whites?

l'équipement d'entretien • cleaning equipment

le tuyau flexible
suction hose

la balayette
brush

la pelle
dust pan

l'eau de Javel
bleach

le seau
bucket

la poudre
powder

le liquide
liquid

le chiffon
duster

l'aspirateur
vacuum cleaner

le balai laveur
mop

le détergent
detergent

la cire
polish

les activités • activities

nettoyer
clean (v)

laver
wash (v)

essuyer
wipe (v)

laver à la brosse
scrub (v)

racler
scrape (v)

le balai
broom

balayer
sweep (v)

épousseter
dust (v)

cirer
polish (v)

français • english

l'atelier • workshop

le mandrin
chuck

la mèche
drill bit

la pile
battery pack

la scie sauteuse
jigsaw

la perceuse rechargeable
rechargeable drill

la perceuse électrique
electric drill

le pistolet à colle
glue gun

le serre-joint
clamp

la lame
blade

l'étau
vice

la ponceuse
sander

la scie circulaire
circular saw

l'établi
workbench

la colle à bois
wood glue

le porte-outils
tool rack

la guimbarde
router

le vilebrequin
bit brace

les copeaux
wood shavings

la rallonge
extension lead

les techniques • techniques

découper
cut (v)

scier
saw (v)

percer
drill (v)

marteler
hammer (v)

raboter
plane (v)

tourner
turn (v)

la soudure
solder

sculpter
carve (v)

souder
solder (v)

les matériaux • materials

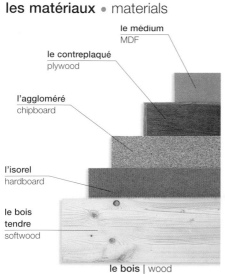

le médium
MDF

le contreplaqué
plywood

l'aggloméré
chipboard

l'isorel
hardboard

**le bois
tendre**
softwood

le bois | wood

le bois dur
hardwood

le vernis
varnish

**la couleur
pour bois**
woodstain

le fil de fer
wire

le câble
cable

l'inox
stainless steel

galvanisé
galvanised

le métal | metal

la boîte à outils • toolbox

la clef
spanner

la clef à molette
adjustable spanner

le marteau
hammer

la pince plate
needle-nose pliers

la clef à pipe
socket wrench

les embouts
de tournevis
screwdriver
bits

le niveau
spirit level

le joint
washer

le tournevis
screwdriver

l'écrou
nut

le mètre
tape measure

le couteau
knife

la pince universelle
bull-nose pliers

la douille
socket

la clef
key

les forets • drill bits

le foret à métaux
metal bit

le foret à bois plat
flat wood bit

le tournevis cruciforme
phillips screwdriver

l'alésoir
reamer

la tête
head

le foret de
sécurité
security bit

le clou
nail

les forets à
bois
carpentry bits

le foret de
maçonnerie
masonry bit

la vis
screw

80

la pince à dénuder
wire strippers

la pince coupante
wire cutters

le fer à souder
soldering iron

le ruban
isolant
insulating
tape

la soudure
solder

le scalpel
scalpel

la scie à
chantourner
fretsaw

la scie à dosseret | tenon saw

les lunettes de
sécurité
safety goggles

le rabot
plane

la boîte à onglets
mitre block

la scie égoïne
handsaw

la scie à métaux
hacksaw

la perceuse
manuelle
hand drill

la paille de fer
wire wool

la clef serre-tube
wrench

le papier de verre
sandpaper

le burin
chisel

la ventouse
plunger

la lime
file

la pierre à
aiguiser
sharpening stone

le coupe-tube | pipe cutter

la décoration • decorating

les ciseaux
scissors

le cutter
craft knife

le fil à plomb
plumb line

le grattoir
scraper

le tapissier
décorateur
decorator

le papier peint
wallpaper

l'escabeau
stepladder

la brosse à
tapisser
wallpaper brush

la table à
encoller
pasting table

la brosse à
encoller
pasting brush

la colle à
tapisser
wallpaper paste

le seau
bucket

tapisser | wallpaper (v)

décoller
strip (v)

mastiquer
fill (v)

poncer
sand (v)

plâtrer | plaster (v)

poser | hang (v)

carreler | tile (v)

français • english

le rouleau
roller

le bac à peinture
paint tray

la peinture
paint

la brosse
brush

le pot de
peinture
paint tin

l'éponge
sponge

le papier
cache
masking tape

le papier de
verre
sandpaper

le bleu
overalls

la couverture de
protection
dustsheet

la térébenthine
turpentine

le mastic
filler

le white-spirit
white spirit

peindre
paint (v)

vocabulaire • vocabulary

le plâtre plaster	**brillant** gloss	**le papier gaufré** embossed paper	**la couche de fond** undercoat	**l'enduit** sealant
le vernis varnish	**mat** mat	**le papier d'apprêt** lining paper	**la dernière couche** top coat	**le solvant** solvent
la peinture mate emulsion	**le pochoir** stencil	**l'apprêt** primer	**l'agent de conservation** preservative	**le mastic** grout

le jardin • garden

les styles de jardin • garden styles

le patio
patio garden

le jardin à la française | formal garden

le jardin paysan
cottage garden

le jardin d'herbes aromatiques
herb garden

le jardin sur le toit
roof garden

la rocaille
rock garden

la cour
courtyard

le jardin d'eau
water garden

les ornements de jardin • garden features

le panier suspendu
hanging basket

le treillis
trellis

la pergola
pergola

le pavé
paving

l'allée
path

le tas de
compost
compost heap

le portail
gate

le parterre
flowerbed

le sol • soil

la terre
topsoil

le sable
sand

la cabane
shed

la serre
greenhouse

la clôture
fence

la chaux
chalk

la pelouse
lawn

le bassin
pond

la haie
hedge

l'arceau
arch

le potager
vegetable
garden

la bordure de plantes
herbacées
herbaceous border

la vase
silt

les planches
decking

la fontaine | fountain

l'argile
clay

les plantes de jardin • garden plants

les genres de plantes • types of plants

annuel
annual

bisannuel
biennial

vivace
perennial

le bulbe
bulb

la fougère
fern

le jonc
rush

le bambou
bamboo

les mauvaises herbes
weeds

l'herbe
herb

la plante aquatique
water plant

l'arbre
tree

le palmier
palm

le conifère
conifer

à feuilles persistantes
evergreen

à feuilles caduques
deciduous

la topiaire
topiary

la plante alpestre
alpine

la plante grasse
succulent

le cactus
cactus

la plante en pot
potted plant

la plante d'ombre
shade plant

la plante grimpante
climber

l'arbuste à fleurs
flowering shrub

la couverture du sol
ground cover

la plante rampante
creeper

ornemental
ornamental

l'herbe
grass

les outils de jardin • garden tools

le balai à gazon
lawn rake

le terreau
compost

les graines
seeds

la cendre d'os
bone meal

la bêche
spade

la fourche
fork

la grande cisaille
long-handled shears

le râteau
rake

la houe
hoe

le gravier
gravel

le sac à herbe
grass bag

le moteur
motor

le bras
handle

le panier de jardinier
trug

**l'écran de
protection**
shield

le support
stand

la tondeuse
trimmer

la tondeuse
lawnmower

la brouette
wheelbarrow

la petite fourche
hand fork

le sécateur
secateurs

les gants de jardinage
gardening gloves

le déplantoir
trowel

la ficelle
twine

les étiquettes
labels

la lame
blade

le germoir
seed tray

les attaches
twist ties

les anneaux
ring ties

les cannes
canes

la cisaille
shears

le tamis
sieve

la scie à main
hand saw

le pesticide
pesticide

le pot à fleurs
plant pot

les bottes
rubber boots

l'arrosage • watering

le vaporisateur
spray gun

l'arroseur
sprinkler

le jet
nozzle

l'arrosoir
watering can

le tuyau d'arrosage
hosepipe

la pomme
rose

le dévidoir de tuyau | hose reel

le jardinage • gardening

la
pelouse
lawn

la haie
hedge

le parterre
flowerbed

la
tondeuse
lawnmower

le tuteur
stake

tondre | mow (v)

gazonner
turf (v)

piquer
spike (v)

ratisser
rake (v)

tailler
trim (v)

bêcher
dig (v)

semer
sow (v)

fumer en surface
top dress (v)

arroser
water (v)

français • english

la canne
cane

palisser
train (v)

enlever les fleurs fanées
deadhead (v)

asperger
spray (v)

la coupe
cutting

greffer
graft (v)

propager
propagate (v)

élaguer
prune (v)

mettre un tuteur
stake (v)

transplanter
transplant (v)

désherber
weed (v)

pailler
mulch (v)

récolter
harvest (v)

vocabulaire • vocabulary

cultiver cultivate (v)	**dessiner** landscape (v)	**fertiliser** fertilize (v)	**tamiser** sieve (v)	**biologique** organic	**le semis** seedling	**le sous-sol** subsoil
soigner tend (v)	**mettre en pot** pot up (v)	**cueillir** pick (v)	**retourner** aerate (v)	**le drainage** drainage	**l'engrais** fertilizer	**l'herbicide** weedkiller

les services
services

les services d'urgence • emergency services

l'ambulance • ambulance

l'ambulance
ambulance

le brancard
stretcher

l'infirmier du SAMU
paramedic

la police • police

le badge
badge

l'uniforme
uniform

la sirène
siren

les feux
lights

la voiture de police
police car

le poste de police
police station

la matraque
truncheon

le pistolet
gun

les menottes
handcuffs

le policier
police officer

vocabulaire • vocabulary

l'inspecteur inspector	**le suspect** suspect	**la plainte** complaint	**l'arrestation** arrest
le crime crime	**l'agression** assault	**l'enquête** investigation	**la cellule** police cell
l'officier de police detective	**les empreintes** fingerprint	**le cambriolage** burglary	**l'accusation** charge

les pompiers • fire brigade

la fumée
smoke

le tuyau
hose

la casque
helmet

les sapeurs-pompiers
fire fighters

la nacelle
cradle

le jet d'eau
water jet

la flèche
boom

l'échelle
ladder

la cabine
cab

l'incendie | fire

le poste d'incendie
fire station

l'escalier de secours
fire escape

la voiture de pompiers
fire engine

le détecteur de
fumée
smoke alarm

l'avertisseur
d'incendie
fire alarm

la hache
axe

l'extincteur
fire extinguisher

la borne
d'incendie
hydrant

| **La police/les pompiers/une ambulance, s'il vous plaît.** I need the police/fire brigade/ambulance. | **Il y a un incendie à…** There's a fire at… | **Il y a eu un accident.** There's been an accident. | **Appelez la police!** Call the police! |

la banque • bank

le client
customer

le guichet
window

le caissier
cashier

les dépliants
leaflets

le comptoir
counter

les fiches de
versement
paying-in slips

la carte bancaire
debit card

le talon
stub

le numéro de
compte
account number

la signature
signature

le montant
amount

**le directeur
d'agence**
bank manager

la carte de crédit
credit card

le carnet de chèques
chequebook

le chèque
cheque

---

vocabulaire • vocabulary

l'épargne savings	l'hypothèque mortgage	le paiement payment	verser pay in (v)	le compte courant current account
l'impôt tax	le découvert overdraft	le prélèvement direct debit	les frais bancaires bank charge	le compte d'épargne savings account
le prêt loan	le taux d'intérêt interest rate	la fiche de retrait withdrawal slip	le virement bancaire bank transfer	le code secret pin number

---

la pièce
coin

le billet
note

l'écran
screen

la fente
card slot

le clavier
key pad

l'argent
money

le distributeur
cash machine

les devises étrangères • foreign currency

le bureau de change
bureau de change

le traveller
traveller's cheque

le taux de change
exchange rate

la finance • finance

le prix des actions
share price

l'agent de la bourse
stockbroker

la conseillère financière
financial advisor

la bourse | stock exchange

vocabulaire • vocabulary

encaisser
cash (v)

les actions
shares

la valeur
denomination

les dividendes
dividends

la commission
commission

le comptable
accountant

l'investissement
investment

le portefeuille
portfolio

les titres
stocks

l'action
equity

Est-ce que je peux changer ça, s'il vous plaît?
Can I change this please?

Quel est le taux de change aujourd'hui?
What's today's exchange rate?

les communications • communications

le postier
postal worker

le guichet
window

la balance
scales

le guichet
counter

la poste | post office

le tampon de la poste
postmark

le timbre
stamp

le code postal
postal code

l'adresse
address

l'enveloppe | envelope

le facteur
postman

vocabulaire • vocabulary

la lettre letter	**l'expéditeur** return address	**la distribution** delivery	**fragile** fragile	**ne pas plier** do not bend (v)
par avion by airmail	**la signature** signature	**le mandat postal** postal order	**le sac postal** mailbag	**dessus** this way up
l'envoi en recommandé registered post	**la levée** collection	**le tarif d'affranchissement** postage	**le télégramme** telegram	**le fax** fax

la boîte aux lettres
postbox

la boîte aux lettres
letterbox

le colis
parcel

le service de messagerie
courier

le téléphone • telephone

le combiné
handset

le répondeur
answering machine

la base
base station

le téléphone sans fil
cordless phone

le visiophone
video phone

**la cabine
téléphonique**
telephone box

le clavier
keypad

le combiné
receiver

les pièces rendues
coin return

le portable
mobile phone

le téléphone à pièces
coin phone

le téléphone à carte
card phone

---

vocabulaire • vocabulary

les renseignements directory enquiries	**répondre** answer (v)	**le téléphoniste** operator	**Pouvez-vous me donner le numéro pour...?** Can you give me the number for...?
le P.C.V. reverse charge call	**le texto** text message	**occupé** engaged/busy	
composer dial (v)	**le message vocal** voice message	**coupé** disconnected	**Quel est l'indicatif pour...?** What is the dialling code for...?

---

l'hôtel • hotel
le hall • lobby

le client
guest

la clef de la chambre
room key

les messages
messages

le casier
pigeonhole

la réceptionniste
receptionist

le registre
register

le comptoir
counter

la réception | reception

les bagages
luggage

le diable
trolley

le porteur
porter

l'ascenseur
lift

le numéro de chambre
room number

les chambres • rooms

la chambre simple
single room

la chambre double
double room

la chambre à deux lits
twin room

la salle de bain privée
private bathroom

les services • services

le plateau à petit déjeuner
breakfast tray

le service de ménage
maid service

le service de blanchisserie
laundry service

le service d'étage | room service

le minibar
mini bar

le restaurant
restaurant

la salle de sport
gym

la piscine
swimming pool

---

vocabulaire • vocabulary

la chambre avec le petit déjeuner
bed and breakfast

la pension complète
full board

la demi-pension
half board

Avez-vous une chambre de libre?
Do you have any vacancies?

J'ai une réservation.
I have a reservation.

Je voudrais une chambre simple.
I'd like a single room.

Je voudrais une chambre pour trois nuits.
I'd like a room for three nights.

C'est combien par nuit?
What is the charge per night?

Quand est-ce que je dois quitter la chambre?
When do I have to vacate the room?

---

les courses
shopping

le centre commercial • shopping centre

l'atrium
atrium

l'enseigne
sign

l'ascenseur
lift

le deuxième
étage
second floor

le premier
étage
first floor

l'escalier
mécanique
escalator

le rez-de-
chaussée
ground floor

le client
customer

vocabulaire • vocabulary

le rayon enfants children's department	**le guide** store directory	**les cabines d'essayage** changing rooms	**C'est combien?** How much is this?
le rayon bagages luggage department	**le vendeur** sales assistant	**les soins de bébés** baby changing facilities	**Est-ce que je peux changer ça?** May I exchange this?
le rayon chaussures shoe department	**le service après-vente** customer services	**les toilettes** toilets	

le grand magasin • department store

les vêtements pour
hommes
men's wear

les vêtement pour
femmes
women's wear

la lingerie
lingerie

la parfumerie
perfumery

la beauté
beauty

le linge de maison
linen

l'ameublement
home furnishings

la mercerie
haberdashery

la vaisselle
kitchenware

la porcelaine
china

l'électroménager
electrical goods

l'éclairage
lighting

les articles de sport
sports

les jouets
toys

la papeterie
stationery

l'alimentation
food hall

le supermarché • supermarket

l'allée
aisle

l'étagère
shelf

le tapis roulant
conveyer belt

le caissier
cashier

les promotions
offers

la caisse | checkout

le client
customer

la caisse
till

la sac à
provisions
shopping bag

les provisions
groceries

l'anse
handle

le code barres
bar code

le caddie
trolley

le panier
basket

le lecteur optique
scanner

la boulangerie
bakery

la crémerie
dairy

les céréales
cereals

les conserves
tinned food

la confiserie
confectionery

les légumes
vegetables

les fruits
fruit

la viande et la
volaille
meat and poultry

le poisson
fish

la charcuterie
deli

les produits
surgelés
frozen food

les plats cuisinés
convenience food

les boissons
drinks

les produits
d'entretien
household products

les articles de
toilette
toiletries

les articles pour
bébés
baby products

l'électroménager
electrical goods

la nourriture pour
animaux
pet food

les magazines | magazines

la pharmacie • chemist

les soins
dentaires
dental care

l'hygiène
féminine
feminine
hygiene

les déodorants
deodorants

les vitamines
vitamins

l'officine
dispensary

le pharmacien
pharmacist

le médicament pour
la toux
cough medicine

l'herboristerie
herbal remedies

les soins de la peau
skin care

l'après-soleil
aftersun

l'écran solaire
sunscreen

l'écran total
sunblock

le produit anti-insecte
insect repellent

la lingette humide
wet wipe

le kleenex
tissue

la serviette hygiénique
sanitary towel

le tampon
tampon

le protège-slip
panty liner

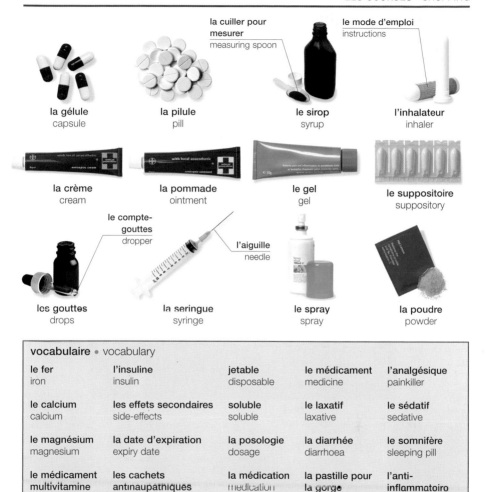

la cuiller pour
mesurer
measuring spoon

le mode d'emploi
instructions

la gélule
capsule

la pilule
pill

le sirop
syrup

l'inhalateur
inhaler

la crème
cream

la pommade
ointment

le gel
gel

le suppositoire
suppository

le compte-
gouttes
dropper

l'aiguille
needle

les gouttes
drops

la seringue
syringe

le spray
spray

la poudre
powder

vocabulaire • vocabulary

le fer iron	**l'insuline** insulin	**jetable** disposable	**le médicament** medicine	**l'analgésique** painkiller
le calcium calcium	**les effets secondaires** side-effects	**soluble** soluble	**le laxatif** laxative	**le sédatif** sedative
le magnésium magnesium	**la date d'expiration** expiry date	**la posologie** dosage	**la diarrhée** diarrhoea	**le somnifère** sleeping pill
le médicament multivitamine multivitamins	**les cachets antinaupathiques** travel sickness pills	**la médication** medication	**la pastille pour la gorge** throat lozenge	**l'anti-inflammatoire** anti-inflammatory

le fleuriste • florist

les fleurs
flowers

le glaïeul
gladiolus

l'iris
iris

le lis
lily

la marguerite
daisy

l'acacia
acacia

le chrysanthème
chrysanthemum

l'œillet
carnation

la gypsophile
gypsophila

la plante en pot
pot plant

la giroflée
stocks

le gerbera
gerbera

le feuillage
foliage

la rose
rose

le freesia
freesia

le vase
vase

l'orchidée
orchid

la pivoine
peony

la botte
bunch

la tige
stem

la jonquille
daffodil

le bourgeon
bud

l'emballage
wrapping

la tulipe | tulip

les compositions florales • arrangements

le ruban
ribbon

le bouquet
bouquet

les fleurs séchées
dried flowers

le pot-pourri | pot-pourri

la couronne | wreath

la guirlande
de fleurs
garland

Je peux y attacher un message? Can I attach a message?	**Elles tiennent combien de temps?** How long will these last?
Est-ce qu'elles sentent bon? Are they fragrant?	**Pouvez-vous les envoyer à…?** Can you send them to….?
Pouvez-vous les emballer? Can I have them wrapped?	**Je voudrais un bouquet de…, SVP.** Can I have a bunch of… please.

le marchand de journaux • newsagent

les cigarettes
cigarettes

le paquet de cigarettes
packet of cigarettes

les allumettes
matches

les billets de loterie
lottery tickets

les timbres
stamps

la carte postale
postcard

la bande dessinée
comic

le magazine
magazine

le journal
newspaper

fumer • smoking

le tuyau
stem

le fourneau
bowl

le tabac
tobacco

le briquet
lighter

la pipe
pipe

le cigare
cigar

le confiseur • confectioner

la boîte de chocolats
box of chocolates

la friandise
snack bar

les chips
crisps

la confiserie | sweet shop

vocabulaire • vocabulary

le chocolat au lait milk chocolate	le caramel caramel
le chocolat noir plain chocolate	la truffe truffle
le chocolat blanc white chocolate	le biscuit biscuit
les bonbons assortis pick and mix	les bonbons boiled sweets

la confiserie • confectionery

le chocolat
chocolate

la tablette de chocolat
chocolate bar

les bonbons
sweets

la sucette
lollipop

le caramel
toffee

le nougat
nougat

la guimauve
marshmallow

le bonbon à la menthe
mint

le chewing-gum
chewing gum

la dragée à la gelée
jellybean

le bonbon au fruit
fruit gum

le réglisse
licquorice

les autres magasins • other shops

la boulangerie
baker's

la pâtisserie
cake shop

la boucherie
butcher's

la poissonnerie
fishmonger's

le marchand de légumes
greengrocer's

l'épicerie
grocer's

le magasin de chaussures
shoe shop

la quincaillerie
hardware shop

le magasin d'antiquités
antiques shop

la boutique de cadeaux
gift shop

l'agence de voyage
travel agent's

la bijouterie
jeweller's

la librairie
book shop

le magasin de disques
record shop

le magasin de vins et spiritueux
off licence

l'animalerie
pet shop

le magasin de meubles
furniture shop

la boutique
boutique

vocabulaire • vocabulary

l'agent immobilier
estate agent's

le magasin d'appareils photos
camera shop

la pépinière
garden centre

le magasin bio
health food shop

le pressing
dry cleaner's

la boutique d'art
art shop

la laverie automatique
launderette

le marchand d'occasion
second-hand shop

le tailleur
tailor's

le salon de coiffure
hairdresser's

le marché | market

la nourriture
food

la viande • meat

l'agneau
lamb

le boucher
butcher

l'allonge
meat hook

la balance
scales

le fusil
knife sharpener

le bacon
bacon

les saucisses
sausages

le foie
liver

vocabulaire • vocabulary

le porc pork	**la venaison** venison	**les abats** offal	**de ferme** free range	**la viande rouge** red meat
le bœuf beef	**le lapin** rabbit	**salé** cured	**naturel** organic	**la viande maigre** lean meat
le veau veal	**la langue de bœuf** tongue	**fumé** smoked	**la viande blanche** white meat	**la viande cuite** cooked meat

les morceaux de viande • cuts

la tranche
slice

le jambon
ham

la couenne
rind

la tranche de lard
rasher

la viande hachée
mince

le filet
fillet

le rumsteck
rump steak

le rognon
kidney

le gras
fat

l'os
bone

le bifteck d'aloyau
sirloin steak

la côte de bœuf
rib

la côtelette
chop

le gigot
joint

le cœur
heart

la volaille • poultry

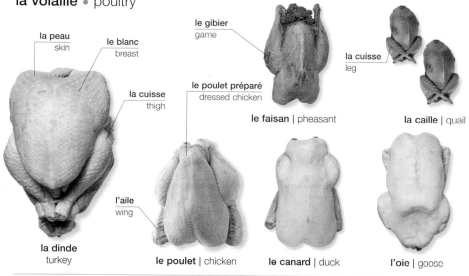

la peau
skin

le blanc
breast

le gibier
game

la cuisse
leg

la cuisse
thigh

le poulet préparé
dressed chicken

le faisan | pheasant

la caille | quail

l'aile
wing

la dinde
turkey

le poulet | chicken

le canard | duck

l'oie | goose

le poisson • fish

les crevettes décortiquées
peeled prawns

le rouget barbet
red mullet

les filets de flétan
halibut fillets

la truite arc-en-ciel
rainbow trout

la glace
ice

les ailes de raie
skate wings

la poissonnerie
fishmonger's

la lotte
monkfish

le maquereau
mackerel

la truite
trout

l'espadon
swordfish

la sole
Dover sole

la limande-sole
lemon sole

l'aiglefin
haddock

la sardine
sardine

la raie
skate

le merlan
whiting

le bar
sea bass

le saumon | salmon

la morue
cod

la daurade
sea bream

le thon
tuna

les fruits de mer • seafood

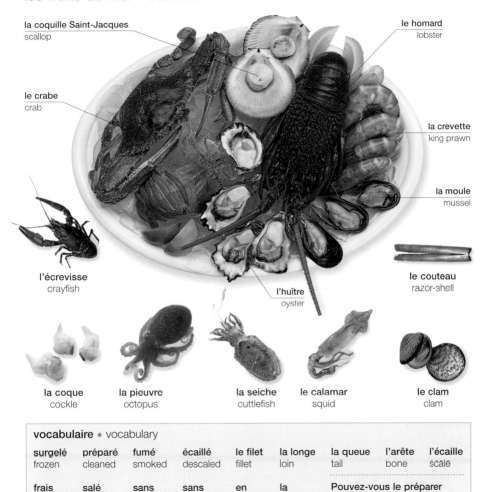

la coquille Saint-Jacques
scallop

le homard
lobster

le crabe
crab

la crevette
king prawn

la moule
mussel

l'écrevisse
crayfish

l'huître
oyster

le couteau
razor-shell

la coque
cockle

la pieuvre
octopus

la seiche
cuttlefish

le calamar
squid

le clam
clam

vocabulaire • vocabulary

surgelé frozen	**préparé** cleaned	**fumé** smoked	**écaillé** descaled	**le filet** fillet	**la longe** loin	**la queue** tail	**l'arête** bone	**l'écaille** scale
frais fresh	**salé** salted	**sans peau** skinned	**sans arêtes** boned	**en filets** filleted	**la tranche** steak	**Pouvez-vous le préparer pour moi?** Will you clean it for me?		

les légumes 1 • vegetables 1

la graine
seed

la fève
broad bean

le haricot grimpant
runner bean

le haricot vert
French bean

le petit pois
garden pea

la gousse
pod

le germe de soja
bean sprout

le bambou
bamboo

l'okra
okra

le maïs
sweetcorn

l'endive
chicory

le fenouil
fennel

les cœurs de palmier
palm hearts

le céleri
celery

---

vocabulaire • vocabulary

la feuille leaf	**la fleurette** floret	**la pointe** tip	**biologique** organic
le trognon stalk	**le grain** kernel	**le cœur** heart	**le sac en plastique** plastic bag

Est-ce que vous vendez des légumes bios?
Do you sell organic vegetables?

Est-ce qu'ils sont cultivés dans la région?
Are these grown locally?

---

la roquette
rocket

le cresson
watercress

le radicchio
radicchio

le chou de Bruxelles
brussel sprout

la bette
swiss chard

le chou frisé
kale

l'oseille
sorrel

la chicorée
endive

le pissenlit
dandelion

les épinards
spinach

le chou-rave
kohlrabi

le chou chinois
pak-choi

la laitue
lettuce

le brocoli
broccoli

le chou
cabbage

le chou précoce
spring greens

les légumes 2 • vegetables 2

l'artichaut
artichoke

le radis
radish

le chou-fleur
cauliflower

le navet
turnip

la pomme
de terre
potato

l'oignon
onion

le poivron
pepper

le piment
chilli

la courge
marrow

---

vocabulaire • vocabulary

la tomate cerise cherry tomato	**le céleri** celeriac	**surgelé** frozen	**amer** bitter	**Puis-je avoir un kilo de pommes de terre s'il vous plaît?** Can I have one kilo of potatoes please?
la carotte carrot	**le taro** taro root	**cru** raw	**ferme** firm	
le fruit de l'arbre à pain breadfruit	**le manioc** cassava	**épicé** hot (spicy)	**la pulpe** flesh	**C'est combien le kilo?** What's the price per kilo?
la pomme de terre nouvelle new potato	**la châtaigne d'eau** water chestnut	**sucré** sweet	**la racine** root	**Ils s'appellent comment?** What are those called?

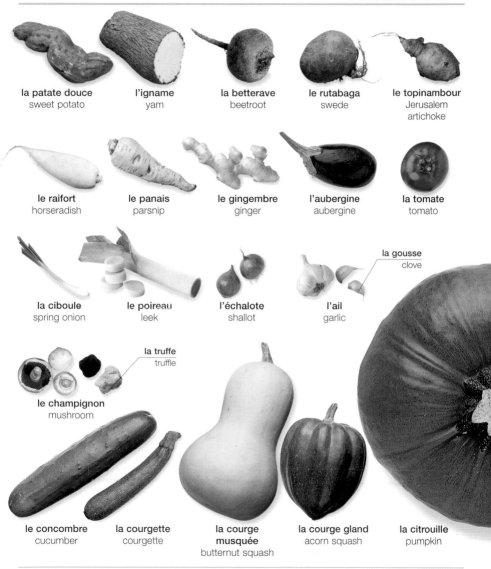

la patate douce
sweet potato

l'igname
yam

la betterave
beetroot

le rutabaga
swede

le topinambour
Jerusalem
artichoke

le raifort
horseradish

le panais
parsnip

le gingembre
ginger

l'aubergine
aubergine

la tomate
tomato

la ciboule
spring onion

le poireau
leek

l'échalote
shallot

l'ail
garlic

la gousse
clove

la truffe
truffle

le champignon
mushroom

le concombre
cucumber

la courgette
courgette

**la courge
musquée**
butternut squash

la courge gland
acorn squash

la citrouille
pumpkin

le fruit 1 • fruit 1

les agrumes • citrus fruit

l'orange
orange

la clémentine
clementine

le tangelo
ugli fruit

**la peau
blanche**
pith

le pamplemousse
grapefruit

le quartier
segment

la mandarine
tangerine

la satsuma
satsuma

le zeste
zest

le citron vert
lime

le citron
lemon

le kumquat
kumquat

les fruits à noyau • stoned fruit

la pêche
peach

la nectarine
nectarine

l'abricot
apricot

la prune
plum

la cerise
cherry

la pomme
apple

la poire
pear

la corbeille de fruits | basket of fruit

les fruits rouges et les melons • berries and melons

la fraise
strawberry

la framboise
raspberry

le melon
melon

les raisins
grapes

la mûre
blackberry

la groseille
redcurrant

l'écorce
rind

la canneberge
cranberry

le cassis
blackcurrant

le pépin
seed

la pulpe
flesh

la myrtille
blueberry

la groseille blanche
white currant

la pastèque
watermelon

la loganberry
loganberry

la groseille à maquereau
gooseberry

vocabulaire • vocabulary

la rhubarbe rhubarb	**aigre** sour	**croquant** crisp	**le jus** juice	**Est-ce qu'ils sont mûrs?** Are they ripe?
la fibre fibre	**frais** fresh	**pourri** rotten	**le trognon** core	**Je peux goûter?** Can I try one?
sucré sweet	**juteux** juicy	**la pulpe** pulp	**sans pépins** seedless	**Ils se gardent combien de temps?** How long will they keep?

les fruits 2 • fruit 2

la mangue
mango

l'ananas
pineapple

l'avocat
avocado

la papaye
papaya

la pêche
peach

le litchi
lychee

le kiwi
kiwifruit

le physalis
cape gooseberry

le pépin
pip

la peau
skin

le coing
quince

le fruit de la passion
passion fruit

la banane
banana

la goyave
guava

la grenade
pomegranate

le kaki
persimmon

le feijoa
feijoa

la figue de Barbarie
prickly pear

la carambole
starfruit

le mangoustan
mangosteen

les noix et les fruits secs • nuts and dried fruit

le pignon
pine nut

la pistache
pistachio

la noix de cajou
cashewnut

la cacahouète
peanut

la noisette
hazelnut

la noix du Brésil
brazilnut

la noix pacane
pecan

l'amande
almond

la noix
walnut

le marron
chestnut

la coquille
shell

le macadamia
macadamia

la figue
fig

la datte
date

le pruneau
prune

la chair
flesh

le raisin de Smyrne
sultana

le raisin sec
raisin

le raisin de Corinthe
currant

la noix de coco
coconut

vocabulaire • vocabulary

vert green	**dur** hard	**l'amande** kernel	**salé** salted	**grillé** roasted	**décortiqué** shelled	**le fruit confit** candied fruit
mûr ripe	**mou** soft	**séché** desiccated	**cru** raw	**de saison** seasonal	**complet** whole	**les fruits tropicaux** tropical fruit

les céréales et les légumes secs • grains and pulses

les céréales • grains

le blé
wheat

l'avoine
oats

l'orge
barley

le millet
millet

le maïs
corn

le quinoa
quinoa

vocabulaire • vocabulary		
la graine seed	**parfumé** fragranced	**facile à** **cuisiner** easy cook
la balle husk	**la céréale** cereal	**à grains** **longs** long-grain
le grain kernel	**complet** wholegrain	
sec dry	**laisser** **tremper** soak (v)	**à grains** **ronds** short-grain
frais fresh		

le riz • rice

le riz blanc
white rice

le riz complet
brown rice

le riz sauvage
wild rice

le riz rond
pudding rice

les céréales traitées • processed grains

le couscous
couscous

le blé écrasé
cracked wheat

la semoule
semolina

le son
bran

les haricots et les pois • beans and peas

les gros haricots blancs
butter beans

les haricots blancs
haricot beans

les haricots rouges
red kidney beans

les adzukis
aduki beans

les fèves
broad beans

les graines de soja
soya beans

les haricots à œil noir
black-eyed beans

les haricots pinto
pinto beans

les haricots mung
mung beans

les flageolets
flageolet beans

les lentilles
brown lentils

les lentilles rouges
red lentils

les petits pois
green peas

les pois chiches
chick peas

les pois cassés
split peas

les graines • seeds

la graine de potiron
pumpkin seed

le grain de moutarde
mustard seed

la graine de carvi
caraway

la graine de sésame
sesame seed

la graine de tournesol
sunflower seed

les herbes et les épices • herbs and spices

les épices • spices

la vanille
vanilla

la noix de muscade
nutmeg

le macis
mace

le curcuma
turmeric

le cumin
cumin

le bouquet garni
bouquet garni

le poivre de la Jamaïque
allspice

le grain de poivre
peppercorn

le fenugrec
fenugreek

le piment
chilli

en morceaux
whole

écrasé
crushed

le safran
saffron

la cardamome
cardamom

la poudre de curry
curry powder

en poudre
ground

le paprika
paprika

en flocons
flakes

l'ail
garlic

les herbes • herbs

les bâtons
sticks

la cannelle
cinnamon

la citronnelle
lemon grass

le clou de girofle
cloves

l'anis étoilé
star anise

le gingembre
ginger

le fenouil
fennel

les graines de fenouil
fennel seeds

la ciboulette
chives

l'estragon
tarragon

l'origan
oregano

la menthe
mint

la marjolaine
marjoram

la coriandre
coriander

la feuille de laurier
bay leaf

le thym
thyme

le basilic
basil

l'aneth
dill

le persil
parsley

la sauge
sage

le romarin
rosemary

les aliments en bouteilles • bottled foods

l'huile de noix
walnut oil

l'huile de pépins
de raisin
grapeseed oil

le bouchon
cork

l'huile de
tournesol
sunflower oil

l'huile
d'amande
almond oil

l'huile de
sésame
sesame
seed oil

l'huile de noisette
hazelnut oil

l'huile d'olive
olive oil

les herbes
herbs

l'huile parfumée
flavoured oil

les huiles
oils

les produits à tartiner • sweet spreads

le pot
jar

le gâteau de miel
honeycomb

le miel solide
set honey

la pâte à tartiner au citron	la confiture de framboises	la confiture d'oranges	le miel liquide	le sirop d'érable
lemon curd	raspberry jam	marmalade	clear honey	maple syrup

les condiments • condiments and spreads

le vinaigre de
cidre
cider vinegar

le vinaigre
balsamique
balsamic vinegar

la bouteille
bottle

la moutarde
anglaise
English mustard

la mayonnaise
mayonnaise

le ketchup
ketchup

la moutarde
française
French mustard

le vinaigre de malt
malt vinegar

le vinaigre de vin
wine vinegar

la sauce
sauce

la moutarde
en grains
wholegrain
mustard

le chutney
chutney

le vinaigre
vinegar

le bocal scellé
sealed jar

**le beurre de
cacahouètes**
peanut butter

**la pâte à tartiner
au chocolat**
chocolate spread

**les fruits en
bocaux**
preserved fruit

vocabulaire • vocabulary

l'huile de maïs
corn oil

l'huile de colza
rapeseed oil

**l'huile
d'arachide**
groundnut oil

**l'huile pressée
à froid**
cold-pressed oil

l'huile végétale
vegetable oil

les produits laitiers • dairy produce

le fromage • cheese

le fromage à pâte
pressée non cuite
semi-hard cheese

le fromage râpé
grated cheese

la croûte
rind

le fromage à pâte pressée cuite
hard cheese

le fromage à pâte
semi-molle
semi-soft cheese

le cottage
cottage
cheese

le fromage à
la crème
cream cheese

le bleu
blue cheese

le fromage à pâte molle
soft cheese

le fromage frais | fresh cheese

le lait • milk

le lait
entier
whole milk

le lait demi-écrémé
semi-skimmed milk

le lait écrémé
skimmed milk

le carton de lait
milk carton

le lait de
chèvre
goat's milk

le lait condensé
condensed milk

le lait de vache | cow's milk

le beurre
butter

la margarine
margarine

la crème
cream

la crème allégée
single cream

la crème épaisse
double cream

la crème fouettée
whipped cream

la crème fraîche
sour cream

le yaourt
yoghurt

la glace
ice-cream

les œufs • eggs

le jaune d'œuf
yolk

le blanc d'œuf
egg white

la coquille
shell

le coquetier
egg cup

l'œuf à la coque
boiled egg

l'œuf de poule
hen's egg

l'œuf de cane
duck egg

l'œuf d'oie
goose egg

l'œuf de caille
quail egg

---

vocabulaire • vocabulary

pasteurisé pasteurized	**le milk-shake** milkshake	**salé** salted	**le lait de brebis** sheep's milk	**le lactose** lactose	**homogénéisé** homogenised
non pasteurisé unpasteurized	**le yaourt surgelé** frozen yoghurt	**non salé** unsalted	**le babeurre** buttermilk	**sans matières grasses** fat free	**le lait en poudre** powdered milk

les pains et la farine • breads and flours

le pain tranché
sliced bread

les graines de pavot
poppy seeds

le pain de seigle
rye bread

la baguette
baguette

la boulangerie | bakery

faire du pain • making bread

la farine blanche
white flour

la farine complète
brown flour

la farine brute
wholemeal flour

la levure
yeast

tamiser | sift (v)

mélanger | mix (v)

la pâte
dough

faire cuire au four | bake (v)

français • english

la croûte
crust

le pain
loaf

la tranche
slice

le pain blanc
white bread

le pain bis
brown bread

le pain de son
wholemeal bread

le pain complet
granary bread

le pain de maïs
corn bread

le pain au bicarbonate de soude
soda bread

le pain au levain
sourdough bread

le pain plat
flatbread

le petit pain américain
bagel

le petit pain rond
bap

le petit pain
roll

le pain aux raisins secs
fruit bread

le pain aux graines
seeded bread

le naan
naan bread

le pita
pitta bread

le biscuit scandinave
crispbread

---

vocabulaire • vocabulary

la farine traitée strong flour	**se lever** rise (v)	**lever** prove (v)	**la chapelure** breadcrumbs	**la machine à couper** slicer
la farine avec la levure self-raising flour	**la farine sans levure** plain flour	**glacer** glaze (v)	**la flûte** flute	**le boulanger** baker

les gâteaux et les desserts • cakes and desserts

l'éclair
éclair

la pâte à choux
choux pastry

la pâte feuilletée
puff pastry

la crème
cream

la pâte de filo
filo pastry

la garniture
filling

enrobé de chocolat
chocolate coated

le cake
fruit cake

le muffin
muffin

la tarte aux fruits
fruit tart

la madeleine
sponge cake

la meringue
meringue

les gâteaux | cakes

---

vocabulaire • vocabulary

la crème pâtissière crème patisserie	**le petit gâteau** bun	**la pâte** pastry	**le riz au lait** rice pudding	**Est-ce que je peux avoir une tranche s'il vous plaît?** May I have a slice please?
le gâteau au chocolat chocolate cake	**la crème anglaise** custard	**la tranche** slice	**la fête** celebration	

---

les pépites de chocolat
chocolate chip

les boudoirs
sponge fingers

le florentine
florentine

le diplomate
trifle

les biscuits | biscuits

la mousse
mousse

le sorbet
sorbet

la tarte à la crème
cream pie

la crème caramel
crème caramel

les gâteaux de fête • celebration cakes

l'étage supérieur
top tier

le ruban
ribbon

l'étage inférieur
bottom tier

le glaçage
icing

la pâte d'amandes
marzipan

le gâteau de mariage | wedding cake

la décoration
decoration

les bougies d'anniversaire
birthday candles

souffler
blow out (v)

le gâteau d'anniversaire | birthday cake

la charcuterie • delicatessen

le saucisson piquant
spicy sausage

l'huile
oil

le vinaigre
vinegar

la viande non cuite
uncooked meat

le comptoir
counter

le salami
salami

le pepperoni
pepperoni

la quiche
flan

le pâté
pâté

la mozzarella
mozzarella

le brie
brie

le fromage de chèvre
goat's cheese

le cheddar
cheddar

le parmesan
parmesan

le camembert
camembert

la croûte
rind

l'édam
edam

le manchego
manchego

les pâtés en croûte
pies

l'olive noire
black olive

le piment
chili

la sauce
sauce

le petit pain
bread roll

la viande cuite
cooked meat

l'olive verte
green olive

le jambon
ham

le comptoir sandwichs
sandwich counter

le poisson fumé
smoked fish

les câpres
capers

le chorizo
chorizo

le prosciutto
prosciutto

l'olive fourrée
stuffed olive

vocabulaire • vocabulary

à l'huile in oil	**mariné** marinated	**fumé** smoked
en saumure in brine	**salé** salted	**séché** cured

Prenez un numéro, s'il vous plaît.
Take a number please.

Est-ce que je peut goûter un peu de ça, s'il vous plaît?
Can I try some of that please?

Je voudrais six tranches, s'il vous plaît.
May I have six slices of that please?

les boissons • drinks

l' eau • water

l'eau en bouteille
bottled water

gazeux
sparkling

non gazeux
still

l'eau minérale
mineral water

l'eau du robinet
tap water

le tonic
tonic water

le soda
soda water

les boissons chaudes • hot drinks

le sachet de thé
teabag

les feuilles de thé
loose leaf tea

le thé
tea

les grains
beans

le café moulu
ground coffee

le café
coffee

le chocolat chaud
hot chocolate

la boisson maltée
malted drink

les boissons non alcoolisées • soft drinks

la paille
straw

le jus de tomate
tomato juice

le jus de raisin
grape juice

la limonade
lemonade

l'orangeade
orangeade

le coca
cola

les boissons alcoolisées • alcoholic drinks

la boîte
can

le gin
gin

la bière
beer

le cidre
cider

la bière anglaise
bitter

la bière brune
stout

la vodka
vodka

le whisky
whisky

le rhum
rum

le brandy
brandy

sec
dry

rosé
rosé

blanc
white

rouge
red

le porto
port

le sherry
sherry

le campari
campari

la liqueur
liqueur

la téquila
tequila

le champagne
champagne

le vin
wine

sortir manger
eating out

le café • café

le store
awning

le menu
menu

le parasol
umbrella

la terrasse de café
terrace café

le serveur
waiter

le percolateur
coffee machine

la table
table

la terrasse de café | pavement café

le snack | snack bar

le café • coffee

le crème
white coffee

le noir
black coffee

le chocolat en
poudre
cocoa powder

la mousse
froth

le café filtre
filter coffee

l'expresso
espresso

le cappuccino
cappuccino

le café glacé
iced coffee

le thé • tea

la tisane
herbal tea

la camomille
camomile tea

le thé vert
green tea

le thé au lait	le thé nature	le thé au citron	l'infusion de menthe	le thé glacé
tea with milk	black tea	tea with lemon	mint tea	iced tea

les jus et milk-shakes • juices and milkshakes

le milk-shake au chocolat
chocolate milkshake

le milk-shake à la fraise
strawberry milkshake

le milk-shake au café
coffee milkshake

le jus d'orange	le jus de pomme	le jus d'ananas	le jus de tomate
orange juice	apple juice	pineapple juice	tomato juice

la nourriture • food

le pain bis
brown bread

la boule
scoop

le sandwich grillé	la salade	la glace	la pâtisserie
toasted sandwich	salad	ice cream	pastry

français • english

le bar • bar

les verres
glasses

la mesure
optic

la caisse
till

le barman
bartender

la pompe à bière
beer tap

le percolateur
coffee machine

le seau à glace | ice bucket

le tabouret de bar | bar stool

le cendrier | ashtray

le dessous de verre | coaster

le comptoir | bar counter

l'ouvre-bouteille
bottle opener

le levier
lever

le tire-bouchon | corkscrew

les pinces
tongs

l'agitateur
stirrer

le verre gradué
measure

le shaker à cocktails | cocktail shaker

le gin tonic
gin and tonic

le pichet
pitcher

le scotch à l'eau
scotch and water

le glaçon
ice cube

le rhum coca
rum and coke

la vodka à l'orange
vodka and orange

le martini
martini

le cocktail
cocktail

le vin
wine

la bière | beer

un coup
a shot

simple
single

double
double

la mesure
measure

sans glaçons
without ice

citron et glaçons
ice and lemon

avec des glaçons
with ice

---

les amuse-gueule • bar snacks

les chips | crisps

les noix de cajou
cashewnuts

les amandes
almonds

les noix
de cajou
cashewnuts

les cacahouètes
peanuts

les amandes
almonds

les noix | nuts

les olives | olives

---

le restaurant • restaurant

la partie
non-fumeurs
non-smoking
section

la serviette
napkin

le commis
commis chef

le couvert
table
setting

le chef de cuisine
chef

le verre
glass

le plateau
tray

la cuisine
kitchen

le garçon
waiter

---

vocabulaire • vocabulary

le menu du soir evening menu	**les spécialités** specials	**le prix** price	**le pourboire** tip	**le buffet** buffet	**le client** customer
la carte des vins wine list	**à la carte** à la carte	**l'addition** bill	**service compris** service included	**le bar** bar	**le sel** salt
le menu du déjeuner lunch menu	**le plateau de desserts** sweet trolley	**le reçu** receipt	**service non compris** service not included	**la partie fumeurs** smoking section	**le poivre** pepper

---

la carte
menu

commander
order (v)

payer
pay (v)

le menu d'enfant
child's meal

les plats • courses

l'apéritif
apéritif

l'entrée
starter

la soupe
soup

le plat principal
main course

l'accompagnement
side order

la fourchette
fork

la cuiller à café
coffee spoon

le dessert | dessert

le café | coffee

Une table pour deux, s'il vous plaît.
A table for two please.

La carte/la carte des vins, s'il vous plaît.
Can I see the menu/winelist please?

Avez-vous un menu à prix fixe?
Is there a fixed price menu?

Avez vous des plats végétariens?
Do you have any vegetarian dishes?

L'addition/un reçu, s'il vous plaît.
Could I have the bill/a receipt please?

Pouvons-nous payer chacun notre part?
Can we pay separately?

Où sont les toilettes, s'il vous plaît?
Where are the toilets, please?

la restauration rapide • fast food

le hamburger
burger

la paille
straw

**la boisson non-
alcoolisée**
soft drink

les frites
french fries

**la serviette en
papier**
paper napkin

le plateau
tray

le hamburger avec des frites
burger meal

la pizzeria
pizza parlour

le restaurant rapide
burger bar

la carte
menu

manger sur place
eat-in

à emporter
take-away

réchauffer
re-heat (v)

le ketchup
tomato sauce

**À emporter, s'il vous
plaît.**
Can I have that to go
please?

**Est-ce que vous livrez à
domicile?**
Do you deliver?

la pizza
pizza

le tarif
price list

la boisson en boîte
canned drink

la livraison à domicile
home delivery

le marchand de hot-dogs
street stall

le hamburger
hamburger

le petit pan
bun

le hamburger au poulet
chicken burger

le hamburger végétarien
veggie burger

la moutarde
mustard

la saucisse
sausage

le hot-dog
hot dog

le sandwich
sandwich

le sandwich mixte
club sandwich

la garniture
filling

le canapé
open sandwich

le taco
wrap

la sauce
sauce

le kébab
kebab

les beignets de poulet
chicken nuggets

salé
savoury

sucré
sweet

les crêpes | crêpes

la garniture
topping

le poisson avec des frites
fish and chips

les côtes
ribs

le poulet frit
fried chicken

la pizza
pizza

le petit déjeuner • breakfast

le lait
milk

les céréales
cereal

la confiture
jam

les fruit secs
dried fruit

le jambon
ham

le fromage
cheese

le biscuit
scandinave
crispbread

le buffet du petit déjeuner
breakfast buffet

**la confiture
d'oranges**
marmalade

le pâté
pâté

le beurre
butter

le jus de fruit
fruit juice

le café
coffee

le chocolat chaud
hot chocolate

le croissant
croissant

le thé
tea

la table du petit déjeuner | breakfast table

les boissons | drinks

la tomate
tomato

le boudin
black pudding

le toast
toast

la saucisse
sausage

l'œuf sur le plat
fried egg

le bacon
bacon

la brioche
brioche

le pain
bread

le petit déjeuner anglais
English breakfast

le jaune d'œuf
yolk

les kippers
kippers

le pain perdu
french toast

l'œuf à la coque
boiled egg

les œufs brouillés
scrambled eggs

la crème
cream

le yaourt aux fruits
fruit yoghurt

les crêpes
pancakes

les gaufres
waffles

le porridge
porridge

les fruits
fresh fruit

le repas • dinner

le potage | soup

le bouillon | broth

le ragoût | stew

le curry | curry

le rôti
roast

la tourte
pie

le soufflé
soufflé

le chiche-kébab
kebab

les boulettes de viande
meatballs

l'omelette
omelette

les nouilles
noodles

le sauté | stir fry

les pâtes | pasta

le riz
rice

la salade composée
mixed salad

la salade verte
green salad

la vinaigrette
dressing

la préparation • techniques

farci | stuffed

en sauce | **in sauce**

grillé | grilled

mariné | marinated

poché | poached

en purée | mashed

cuit | baked

sauté | pan fried

frit
fried

macéré
pickled

fumé
smoked

frit
deep fried

au sirop
in syrup

assaisonné
dressed

cuit à la vapeur
steamed

séché
cured

l'étude
study

l'école • school

l'institutrice
teacher

le tableau
blackboard

la salle de classe | classroom

l'écolier
schoolboy

l'élève
pupil

l'uniforme
school uniform

le pupitre
desk

le cartable
school bag

la craie
chalk

l'écolière
schoolgirl

---

vocabulaire • vocabulary

l'histoire history	**les sciences** science	**la physique** physics
les langues languages	**l'art/le dessin** art	**la chimie** chemistry
la littérature literature	**la musique** music	**la biologie** biology
la géographie geography	**les mathématiques** maths	**l'éducation physique** physical education

les activités • activities

lire | read (v)

écrire | write (v)

épeler
spell (v)

dessiner
draw (v)

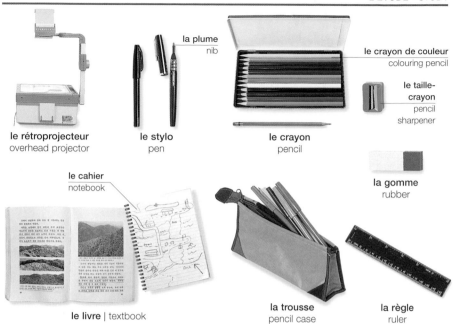

la plume
nib

le crayon de couleur
colouring pencil

le taille-crayon
pencil
sharpener

le rétroprojecteur
overhead projector

le stylo
pen

le crayon
pencil

la gomme
rubber

le cahier
notebook

le livre | textbook

la trousse
pencil case

la règle
ruler

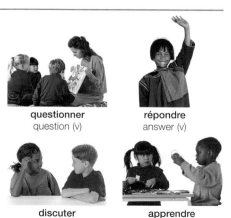

questionner
question (v)

répondre
answer (v)

discuter
discuss (v)

apprendre
learn (v)

vocabulaire • vocabulary		
le directeur head teacher	**la réponse** answer	**la note** grade
la leçon lesson	**les devoirs** homework	**la classe** year
la question question	**l'examen** examination	**le dictionnaire** dictionary
prendre des notes take notes (v)	**la rédaction** essay	**l'encyclopédie** encyclopedia

les mathématiques • maths

les formes • shapes

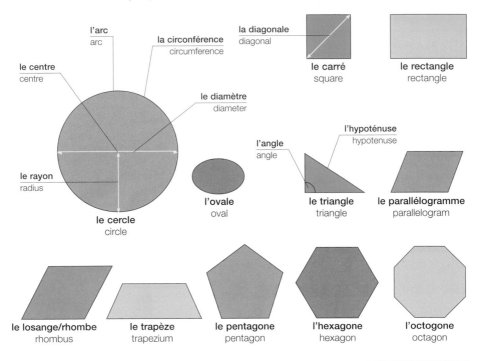

l'arc
arc

la circonférence
circumference

le centre
centre

la diagonale
diagonal

le carré
square

le rectangle
rectangle

le diamètre
diameter

l'hypoténuse
hypotenuse

l'angle
angle

le rayon
radius

le triangle
triangle

le parallélogramme
parallelogram

l'ovale
oval

le cercle
circle

le losange/rhombe
rhombus

le trapèze
trapezium

le pentagone
pentagon

l'hexagone
hexagon

l'octogone
octagon

les solides • solids

le côté
side

le sommet
apex

la base
base

le cône
cone

le cylindre
cylinder

le cube
cube

la pyramide
pyramid

la sphère
sphere

les lignes • lines

droit	parallèle	perpendiculaire	courbe
straight	parallel	perpendicular	curved

les mesures • measurements

le volume	la fraction	les dimensions	l'aire
volume	fraction	dimensions	area

le numérateur
numerator

le dénominateur
denominator

la largeur
width

la longueur
length

la hauteur
height

la profondeur
depth

l'équipement • equipment

l'équerre	le rapporteur	la règle	le compas	la calculatrice
set square	protractor	ruler	compass	calculator

---

vocabulaire • vocabulary

la géométrie	plus	fois	égale(nt)	additionner	multiplier	l'équation
geometry	plus	times	equals	add (v)	multiply (v)	equation

l'arithmétique	moins	divisé par	compter	soustraire	diviser	le pourcentage
arithmetic	minus	divided by	count (v)	subtract (v)	divide (v)	percentage

---

la science • science

le laboratoire
laboratory

la balance
scales

le poids
weight

la balance à ressort
spring balance

le creuset
crucible

le bec Bunsen
bunsen burner

le trépied
tripod

le statif
clamp stand

la bouteille
glass bottle

l'entonnoir
funnel

la pince
clamp

le bouchon
stopper

la fiole
flask

l'expérience | experiment

l'éprouvette
test tube

le support
rack

le chronomètre
timer

la boîte de Pétri
petri dish

le thermomètre
thermometer

la seringue
syringe

la pince fine
tweezers

le scalpel
scalpel

le compte-gouttes
dropper

le forceps | forceps

la pince
tongs

la spatule
spatula

le pilon
pestle

le mortier
mortar

le papier filtre
filter paper

les lunettes de protection
safety goggles

l'oculaire
eyepiece

le bouton de mise au point
focusing knob

la lentille de l'objectif
objective lens

la platine
stage

la tige de verre
glass rod

la pipette
pipette

le bécher
beaker

le porte-objet
slide

le miroir
mirror

l'aimant
magnet

la pince crocodile
crocodile clip

l'électrode négative
negative electrode

l'électrode positive
positive electrode

le microscope | microscope

la pile | battery

l'enseignement supérieur • college

le secrétariat
admissions

le restaurant
universitaire
refectory

le service
de santé
health centre

le terrain
de sport
sports field

la résidence
universitaire
hall of
residence

le campus | campus

le catalogue
catalogue

la bibliothécaire
librarian

le service de prêt
loans desk

les rayons
bookshelf

le périodique
periodical

la revue
journal

la bibliothèque | library

---

vocabulaire • vocabulary

la carte de lecteur library card	**les renseignements** enquiries	**le prêt** loan
la salle de lecture reading room	**emprunter** borrow (v)	**le livre** book
les ouvrages recommandés reading list	**réserver** reserve (v)	**le titre** title
la date de retour return date	**renouveler** renew (v)	**le couloir** aisle

---

l'étudiant
undergraduate

l'assistant
lecturer

la licenciée
graduate

la robe
robe

la salle de cours
lecture theatre

la cérémonie de la remise des diplômes
graduation ceremony

les écoles • schools

le modèle
model

l'école des beaux arts
art college

le Conservatoire
music school

l'école de danse
dance academy

vocabulaire • vocabulary

la bourse scholarship	**la recherche** research	**la dissertation** dissertation	**la médecine** medicine	**la philosophie** philosophy
le diplôme diploma	**la maîtrise** masters	**l'U.F.R.** department	**la zoologie** zoology	**la littérature** literature
la licence degree	**le doctorat** doctorate	**le droit** law	**la physique** physics	**l'histoire d'art** history of art
de troisième cycle postgraduate	**la thèse** thesis	**les études d'ingénieur** engineering	**les sciences politiques** politics	**les sciences économiques** economics

le travail
work

le bureau 1 • office 1
le bureau • office

le moniteur
monitor

le porte-crayons
desktop organizer

le classeur
file

la corbeille arrivée
in-tray

l'ordinateur
computer

la corbeille départ
out-tray

le clavier
keyboard

le carnet
notebook

le téléphone
telephone

l'étiquette
label

le bureau
desk

la corbeille à papier
wastebasket

la chaise tournante
swivel chair

le meuble à tiroirs
drawer unit

le tiroir
drawer

le meuble-classeur
filing cabinet

l'équipement de bureau • office equipment

le magasin à papier
paper tray

le guide
paper guide

le fax
fax

l'imprimante | printer

le fax | fax machine

les fournitures de bureau • office supplies

la fiche
compliments
compliments slip

l'en-tête
letterhead

l'enveloppe
envelope

le dossier-classeur
box file

la fiche intercalaire
divider

l'étiquette
tab

le clipboard
clipboard

le bloc-notes
note pad

le dossier suspendu
hanging file

le porte-dossiers
concertina file

le classeur à
levier
lever arch file

les agrafes
staples

le scotch
sticky tape

le tampon encreur
ink pad

l'agenda
personal organizer

l'agrafeuse
stapler

**le dévidoir de
scotch**
tape dispenser

le perforateur
hole punch

le cachet
rubber stamp

l'élastique
rubber band

la pince à dessin
bulldog clip

le trombone
paper clip

la punaise
drawing pin

le panneau d'affichage | notice board

le bureau 2 • office 2

le tableau à feuilles
mobiles
flipchart

le chevalet
easel

la proposition
proposal

le directeur
manager

le compte
rendu
minutes

le rapport
report

le cadre
executive

le réunion | meeting

vocabulaire • vocabulary

la salle de conférence meeting room	**assister à** attend (v)
l'ordre du jour agenda	**présider** chair (v)

La conférence est à quelle heure?
What time is the meeting?

Quelles sont vos heures de bureau?
What are your office hours?

le conférencier
speaker

le projecteur
projector

la présentation | presentation

les affaires • business

le portable
laptop

les notes
notes

l'homme d'affaires
businessman

la femme d'affaires
businesswoman

le déjeuner d'affaires
business lunch

le voyage d'affaires
business trip

le client
client

le rendez-vous
appointment

l'ordinateur de poche
palmtop

l'agenda | diary

le directeur général
managing director

le contrat
business deal

vocabulaire • vocabulary

la société company	**le personnel** staff	**la comptabilité** accounts department	**le service du contentieux** legal department
le siège social head office	**le salaire** salary	**le service marketing** marketing department	**le service après-vente** customer service department
la succursale branch	**le livre de paie** payroll	**le service des ventes** sales department	**le service de ressources humaines** personnel department

l'ordinateur • computer

l'imprimante
printer

le moniteur
monitor

l'écran
screen

l'unité centrale
central processing
unit

le scanneur
scanner

le haut-parleur
speaker

la touche
key

le clavier
keyboard

la souris
mouse

le matériel
hardware

le disque
disk

le portable
laptop

le disque dur
hard drive

le modem
modem

vocabulaire • vocabulary		
la mémoire memory	**le logiciel** software	**le serveur** server
la RAM RAM	**l'application** application	**le port** port
les bytes bytes	**le programme** program	**le processeur** processor
le système system	**le réseau** network	**le câble** **électrique** power cable

le bureau • desktop

la barre de menus
menubar

la barre d'outils
toolbar

le papier peint
wallpaper

la police
font

l'icône
icon

la barre de défilement
scrollbar

la fenêtre
window

le fichier
file

le dossier
folder

la poubelle
trash

---

l'internet • internet

le courrier électronique • email

le navigateur
browser

la boîte de
réception
inbox

le site web
website

naviguer
browse (v)

l'adresse de courrier électronique
email address

---

vocabulaire • vocabulary

connecter connect (v)	**le fournisseur d'accès** service provider	**entrer** log on (v)	**télécharger** download (v)	**envoyer** send (v)	**sauvegarder** save (v)
installer instal (v)	**le compte de courrier** **électronique** email account	**en ligne** on-line	**la pièce jointe** attachment	**recevoir** receive (v)	**chercher** search (v)

---

les médias • media

le studio de télévision • television studio

le présentateur
presenter

l'éclairage
light

le plateau
set

la caméra
camera

la grue de caméra
camera crane

le cameraman
cameraman

---

vocabulaire • vocabulary

la chaîne channel	les nouvelles news	la presse press	le feuilleton soap	le dessin animé cartoon	en direct live
la **programmation** programming	le **documentaire** documentary	la série **télévisée** television series	le jeu **télévisé** game show	en différé prerecorded	émettre broadcast (v)

---

l'interviewer
interviewer

la reporter
reporter

le télésouffleur
autocue

la présentatrice
newsreader

les acteurs
actors

la perche
sound boom

la claquette
clapper board

le décor de cinéma
film set

la radio • radio

le pupitre de mixage
mixing desk

le microphone
microphone

l'ingénieur du son
sound technician

le studio d'enregistrement | recording studio

vocabulaire • vocabulary

la station de radio radio station	**la fréquence** frequency
le D.J. DJ	**le volume** volume
l'émission broadcast	**régler** tune (v)
la longueur d'ondes wavelength	**les ondes courtes** short wave
les grandes ondes long wave	**les ondes moyennes** medium wave

le droit • law

l'huissier de tribunal
court officer

le témoin
witness

le juge
judge

l'avocat
lawyer

le jury
jury

le banc des jurés
jury box

la salle de tribunal | courtroom

l'accusation
prosecution

le greffier
court official

---

vocabulaire • vocabulary

le cabinet lawyer's office	**l'assignation** summons	**l'acte judiciaire** writ	**la cause** court case
le conseil juridique legal advice	**la déposition** statement	**la date du procès** court date	**l'accusation** charge
le client client	**le mandat** warrant	**le plaidoyer** plea	**l'accusé** accused

---

le sténographe
stenographer

le suspect
suspect

l'accusé
defendant

la défense
defence

le criminel
criminal

le portrait-robot
photofit

le casier judiciaire
criminal record

le gardien de prison
prison guard

la cellule
cell

la prison
prison

vocabulaire • vocabulary

la preuve evidence	coupable guilty	la caution bail	**Je voudrais voir un avocat.** I want to see a lawyer.
le verdict verdict	acquitté acquitted	l'appel appeal	**Où est le palais de justice?** Where is the courthouse?
innocent innocent	la condamnation sentence	la liberté conditionnelle parole	**Est-ce que je peux verser la caution?** Can I post bail?

la ferme 1 • farm 1

les terres cultivées
farmland

la cour de ferme
farmyard

la dépendence
outbuilding

la maison
d'habitation
farmhouse

le champ
field

l'agriculteur/le
fermier
farmer

la grange
barn

le potager
vegetable plot

la haie
hedge

la barrière
gate

la clôture
fence

le pré
pasture

le bétail
livestock

le cultivateur
cultivator

le tracteur | tractor

la moissonneuse-batteuse | combine harvester

français • english

les exploitations agricoles • types of farm

la culture
crop

la ferme de culture
arable farm

la ferme laitière
dairy farm

le troupeau
flock

la ferme d'élevage de moutons
sheep farm

la ferme d'aviculture
poultry farm

la ferme d'élevage porcin
pig farm

le centre de pisciculture
fish farm

l'exploitation fruitière
fruit farm

la vigne
vine

la vigne
vineyard

les activités • actions

le sillon
furrow

labourer
plough (v)

semer
sow (v)

traire
milk (v)

donner à manger
feed (v)

arroser | water (v)

récolter | harvest (v)

vocabulaire • vocabulary

l'herbicide herbicide	**le troupeau** herd	**l'auge** trough
le pesticide pesticide	**le silo** silo	**planter** plant (v)

la ferme 2 • farm 2

les cultures • crops

le blé
wheat

le maïs
corn

l'orge
barley

le colza
rapeseed

le tournesol
sunflower

la balle
bale

le foin
hay

la luzerne
alfalfa

le tabac
tobacco

le riz
rice

le thé
tea

le café
coffee

l'épouvantail
scarecrow

le lin
flax

la canne à sucre
sugarcane

le coton
cotton

le bétail • livestock

le porcelet
piglet

le cochon
pig

le veau
calf

la vache
cow

le taureau
bull

le mouton
sheep

l'agneau
lamb

le chevreau
kid

la chèvre
goat

le poulain
foal

le cheval
horse

l'âne
donkey

le poussin
chick

le poulet
chicken

le coq
cockerel

le dindon
turkey

le caneton
duckling

le canard
duck

l'écurie
stable

l'enclos
pen

le poulailler
chicken coop

la porcherie
pigsty

la construction • construction

l'échafaudage
scaffolding

la palette
pallet

l'échelle
ladder

la fenêtre
window

le chevron
rafter

le chariot de levage
fork-lift truck

le chantier
building site

le linteau
lintel

le mur
wall

la poutre
girder

le casque de
sécurité
hard hat

la ceinture à outils
toolbelt

la poutre
beam

le ciment
cement

construire
build (v)

le maçon
builder

la bétonnière
cement mixer

les matériaux • materials

la brique
brick

le bois
timber

la tuile
roof tile

le bloc de béton
concrete block

les outils • tools

le mortier
mortar

la truelle
trowel

le niveau à bulle
spirit level

le manche
handle

le marteau de forgeron
sledgehammer

la pioche
pickaxe

la pelle
shovel

les machines • machinery

le rouleau compresseur
roller

le tombereau
dumper truck

le support
support

le crochet
hook

la grue | crane

les travaux • roadworks

le macadam goudronné
tarmac

le cône
cone

le marteau-piqueur
pneumatic drill

le revêtement
resurfacing

la pelle mécanique
mechanical digger

les professions 1 • occupations 1

le menuisier
carpenter

l'électricien
electrician

le plombier
plumber

le maçon
builder

le jardinier
gardener

l'aspirateur
vacuum
cleaner

le nettoyeur
cleaner

le mécanicien
mechanic

le boucher
butcher

les
ciseaux
scissors

**la marchande de
poissons**
fishmonger

**le marchand de
légumes**
greengrocer

la fleuriste
florist

le coiffeur
hairdresser

le coiffeur
barber

le bijoutier
jeweller

l'employée de magasin
shop assistant

l'agent immobilier
estate agent

l'opticien
optician

le masque
mask

la dentiste
dentist

le docteur
doctor

la pharmacienne
pharmacist

l'infirmière
nurse

la vétérinaire
vet

le fermier
farmer

le pêcheur
fisherman

la mitrailleuse
machine-gun

le badge
identity badge

le garde
security guard

l'uniforme
uniform

le marin
sailor

le soldat
soldier

le policier
policeman

le pompier
fireman

les professions 2 • occupations 2

l'avocat
lawyer

le comptable
accountant

la maquette
model

l'architecte
architect

le scientifique
scientist

l'institutrice
teacher

le bibliothécaire
librarian

la réceptionniste
receptionist

le sac postal
mailbag

le facteur
postman

le conducteur de bus
bus driver

le camionneur
lorry driver

le chauffeur de taxi
taxi driver

le pilote
pilot

l'hôtesse de l'air
air stewardess

l'agent de voyages
travel agent

la toque
chef's hat

le chef
chef

le tutu
tutu

le musicien
musician

la danseuse
dancer

le comédien
actor

la chanteuse
singer

la serveuse
waitress

le barman
barman

le sportif
sportsman

le sculpteur
sculptor

la peintre
painter

le photographe
photographer

le présentateur
newsreader

les notes
notes

le journaliste
journalist

la rédactrice
editor

la dessinatrice
designer

la couturière
seamstress

le couturier
tailor

le transport
transport

les routes • roads

l'autoroute
motorway

le poste de
péage
toll booth

les signalisations
road markings

la bretelle
d'accès
slip road

à sens unique
one-way

l'îlot directionnel
divider

le carrefour
junction

les feux
traffic light

le camion
lorry

le terre-plein
central reservation

le passage inférieur
underpass

la file de droite
inside lane

la voie centrale
middle lane

la voie de
dépassement
outside lane

la bretelle de sortie
exit ramp

la circulation
traffic

l'autopont
flyover

l'accotement
stabilisé
hard shoulder

le téléphone de
secours
emergency phone

le parking réservé
aux personnes
handicapées
disabled parking

l'embouteillage
traffic jam

le passage clouté
pedestrian
crossing

la carte
map

le parc-mètre
parking meter

l'agent de la
circulation
traffic policeman

vocabulaire • vocabulary

le rond-point roundabout	**garer** park (v)	**remorquer** tow away (v)
la déviation diversion	**doubler** overtake (v)	**la route à quatre voies** dual carriageway
les travaux roadworks	**conduire** drive (v)	**C'est la route pour...?** Is this the road to...?
la glissière de sécurité crash barrier	**faire marche arrière** reverse (v)	**Où peut-on se garer?** Where can I park?

les panneaux routiers • road signs

sens interdit
no entry

**la limitation de
vitesse**
speed limit

danger
hazard

arrêt interdit
no stopping

**interdit de tourner
à droite**
no right turn

le bus • bus

le siège du conducteur
driver's seat

la poignée
handrail

la porte automatique
automatic door

la roue avant
front wheel

le compartiment à bagages
luggage hold

la porte | door

le car | coach

les types de bus • types of buses

le numéro de bus
route number

le conducteur
driver

le bus à deux étages
double-decker bus

le tramway
tram

le trolleybus
trolley bus

le bus scolaire | school bus

la roue arrière
rear wheel

la fenêtre
window

le bouton d'arrêt
stop button

le ticket
bus ticket

la sonnette
bell

la gare routière
bus station

l'arrêt de bus
bus stop

vocabulaire • vocabulary

le prix du ticket
fare

l'accès aux handicapés
wheelchair access

l'horaire
timetable

l'abribus
bus shelter

Vous stoppez à...?
Do you stop at...?

C'est quel bus pour aller à...?
Which bus goes to...?

le minibus
minibus

le bus de touristes | tourist bus

la navette | shuttle bus

la voiture 1 • car 1

l'extérieur • exterior

le rétroviseur
wing mirror

le pare-brise
windscreen

le rétroviseur
rearview mirror

l'essuie-glace
windscreen wiper

la porte
door

le coffre
boot

le capot
bonnet

le clignotant
indicator

le pare-chocs
bumper

le phare
headlight

la roue
wheel

le pneu
tyre

la plaque d'immatriculation
licence plate

les bagages
luggage

la galerie
roofrack

le hayon
tailgate

la ceinture de
sécurité
seat belt

le siège d'enfant
child seat

les modèles • types

la petite voiture
small car

la berline à hayon
hatchback

la berline
saloon

le break
estate

la décapotable
convertible

le cabriolet sport
sports car

la voiture à six places
people carrier

la quatre-quatre
four-wheel drive

la voiture d'époque
vintage

la limousine
limousine

la station-service • petrol station

la pompe
petrol pump

le tarif
price

l'aire de stationnement
forecourt

le compresseur
air supply

vocabulaire • vocabulary		
l'huile oil	**avec plomb** leaded	**le lave-auto** car wash
l'essence petrol	**le diesel** diesel	**l'antigel** antifreeze
sans plomb unleaded	**le garage** garage	**le lave-glace** screenwash

Le plein, s'il vous plaît.
Fill the tank, please.

la voiture 2 • car 2

l'intérieur • interior

le repose-tête
headrest

le verrouillage
door lock

la poignée
handle

le siège arrière
back seat

l'accoudoir
armrest

vocabulaire • vocabulary

à deux portes two-door	**à quatre portes** four-door	**automatique** automatic	**le frein** brake	**l'accélérateur** accelerator
à trois portes three-door	**manuel** manual	**l'allumage** ignition	**l'embrayage** clutch	**la climatisation** air conditioning

Pouvez-vous m'indiquer la route pour…?
Can you tell me the way to…?

Où est le parking?
Where is the car park?

On peut se garer ici?
Can I park here?

les commandes • controls

le volant
steering wheel

le klaxon
horn

le tableau de bord
dashboard

les feux de détresse
hazard lights

le navigateur par satellite
satellite navigation

la conduite à gauche | left-hand drive

le thermomètre
temperature gauge

le compte-tours
rev counter

le compteur
speedometer

la jauge d'essence
fuel gauge

la stéréo
car stereo

l'interrupteur feux
lights switch

la manette de chauffage
heater controls

l'odomètre
odometer

le levier de vitesses
gearstick

l'airbag
air bag

la conduite à droite | right-hand drive

français • english

la voiture 3 • car 3

la mécanique • mechanics

le réservoir de
lave-glace
screen wash reservoir

la jauge d'huile
dipstick

le filtre à air
air filter

le réservoir de liquide de frein
brake fluid reservoir

la batterie
battery

la
carrosserie
bodywork

le réservoir de liquide de
refroidissement
coolant reservoir

la culasse
cylinder head

le tuyau
pipe

le toit ouvrant
sunroof

le radiateur
radiator

le ventilateur
fan

le moteur
engine

l'enjoliveur
hubcap

la **boîte de
vitesses**
gearbox

la transmission
transmission

**l'arbre de
transmission**
driveshaft

la crevaison • puncture

la roue de secours
spare tyre

la manivelle
wrench

les écrous de roue
wheel nuts

le cric
jack

changer une roue
change a wheel (v)

le toit
roof

la suspension
suspension

le silencieux
silencer

le pot d'échappement
exhaust pipe

vocabulaire • vocabulary

l'accident de voiture
car accident

le turbocompresseur
turbocharger

la panne
breakdown

le distributeur
distributor

l'assurance
insurance

le châssis
chassis

la dépanneuse
tow truck

le frein à main
handbrake

le mécanicien
mechanic

l'alternateur
alternator

la pression des
pneus
tyre pressure

la courroie de
cames
cam belt

le porte-fusibles
fuse box

**Ma voiture est en
panne.**
I've broken down.

la bougie
spark plug

**Ma voiture ne
démarre pas.**
My car won't start.

la courroie de
ventilateur
fan belt

**Faites-vous les
réparations?**
Do you do repairs?

le réservoir
d'essence
petrol tank

Le moteur chauffe
The engine is
overheating

le réglage de
l'allumage
timing

la moto • motorbike

le casque
helmet

le clignotant
indicator

le compteur
speedometer

l'embrayage
clutch

le frein
brake

le klaxon
horn

l'accélérateur
throttle

les commandes
controls

le porte-bagages
carrier

le réflecteur
reflector

le siège arrière
pillion

la selle
seat

le moteur
engine

le réservoir
d'essence
fuel tank

le feu arrière
tail light

le pot
d'échappement
exhaust pipe

le silencieux
silencer

le réservoir d'huile
oil tank

la boîte de vitesses
gearbox

le filtre d'air
air filter

français • english

les types • types

la visière
visor

le vêtement en cuir
leathers

la bande fluorescente
reflector strap

la genouillère
knee pad

les vêtements | clothing

le phare
headlight

la suspension
suspension

le garde-boue
mudguard

la pédale de frein
brake pedal

l'essieu
axle

le pneu
tyre

la moto de course | racing bike

le pare-brise
windshield

la moto routière | tourer

la moto tout-terrain | dirt bike

la béquille
stand

le scooter | scooter

la bicyclette • bicycle

la selle
saddle

le tube porte-selle
seat post

la bouteille
d'eau
water bottle

le cadre
frame

le frein
brake

le moyeu
hub

les vitesses
gears

la jante
rim

le pneu
tyre

la chaîne
chain

la pédale
pedal

la roue dentée
cog

le tandem
tandem

le vélo de course
racing bike

le vélo tout-terrain
mountain bike

le vélo de randonnée
touring bike

le vélo de ville
road bike

le casque
helmet

la piste cyclable | cycle lane

la barre
crossbar

le guidon
handlebar

le levier de vitesse
gear lever

le levier de frein
brake lever

le démonte-pneu
tyre lever

la rustine
patch

la boîte d'outils | repair kit

la fourche
fork

la clef
key

le rayon
spoke

la pompe
pump

l'antivol
lock

la roue
wheel

la chambre à air
inner tube

le siège d'enfant
child seat

la valve
valve

la bande de roulement
tread

vocabulaire • vocabulary

le phare lamp	la béquille kickstand	le patin de frein brake block	le panier basket	le cale-pied toe clip	freiner brake (v)
le feu arrière rear light	la galerie à vélo bike rack	le câble cable	la dynamo dynamo	la lanière toe strap	faire du vélo cycle (v)
le cataphote reflector	les roues d'entraînement stabilisers	le pignon sprocket	la crevaison puncture	pédaler pedal (v)	changer de vitesse change gear (v)

le train • train

la voiture
carriage

le quai
platform

le caddie
trolley

le numéro de
voie
platform number

le voyageur
commuter

la gare | train station

les types de trains • types of train

la locomotive
engine

la cabine du
conducteur
driver's cab

le rail
rail

le train à vapeur
steam train

le train diesel | diesel train

le train électrique
electric train

le train à grande vitesse
high-speed train

le monorail
monorail

le métro
underground train

le tram
tram

le train de marchandises
freight train

le porte-bagages
luggage rack

la fenêtre
window

la voie ferrée
track

la porte
door

le siège
seat

le compartiment
compartment

le portillon
ticket barrier

le haut-parleur
public address system

l'horaire
timetable

le billet
ticket

la voiture-restaurant | dining car

le hall de gare | concourse

le compartiment-couchettes
sleeping compartment

---

vocabulaire • vocabulary

le réseau ferroviaire rail network	**le plan de métro** underground map	**le guichet** ticket office	**le rail conducteur** live rail
le rapide inter-city train	**le retard** delay	**le contrôleur** ticket inspector	**le signal** signal
l'heure de pointe rush hour	**le prix** fare	**changer** change (v)	**la manette de secours** emergency lever

---

l'avion • aircraft

l'avion de ligne • airliner

le nez
nose

le cockpit
cockpit

le réacteur
engine

le fuselage
fuselage

l'aile
wing

la queue
tail

la gouverne
rudder

la sortie
exit

la roue de nez
nosewheel

le train d'atterrissage
landing gear

l'aileron
aileron

la dérive
fin

l'empennage
tailplane

la cabine • cabin

la sortie de secours
emergency exit

l'hôtesse de l'air
flight attendant

le casier à bagages
overhead locker

le ventilateur
air vent

le hublot
window

la liseuse
reading light

le siège
seat

la rangée
row

l'accoudoir
armrest

le couloir
aisle

la tablette
tray-table

le dossier
seat back

la montgolfière
hot-air balloon

l'U.L.M.
microlight

le planeur
glider

le biplan
biplane

l'hélice
propeller

l'avion léger
light aircraft

l'hydravion
sea plane

le jet privé
private jet

l'avion supersonique
supersonic jet

la pale de rotor
rotor blade

le missile
missile

l'hélicoptère
helicopter

le bombardier
bomber

le chasseur
fighter plane

vocabulaire • vocabulary

le pilote pilot	**décoller** take off (v)	**atterrir** land (v)	**la classe économique** economy class	**les bagages à main** hand luggage
le copilote co-pilot	**voler** fly (v)	**l'altitude** altitude	**la classe affaires** business class	**la ceinture de sécurité** seat belt

l'aéroport • airport

l'aire de stationnement
apron

le porte-bagages
baggage trailer

le terminal
terminal

le véhicule de service
service vehicle

la passerelle
walkway

l'avion de ligne | airliner

---

vocabulaire • vocabulary

la piste runway	**le numéro de vol** flight number	**le tapis roulant** carousel	**les vacances** holiday
le vol international international flight	**l'immigration** immigration	**la sécurité** security	**enregistrer** check in (v)
le vol domestique domestic flight	**la douane** customs	**la machine de rayons x** X-ray machine	**la tour de contrôle** control tower
la correspondance connection	**l'excédent de bagages** excess baggage	**la brochure de vacances** holiday brochure	**faire une réservation de vol** book a flight (v)

---

les bagages à main
hand luggage

les bagages
luggage

le chariot
trolley

l'enregistrement des bagages
check-in desk

le visa
visa

le passeport | passport

le contrôle de passeports
passport control

la carte d'embarquement
boarding pass

le billet
ticket

le numéro de la porte d'embarquement
gate number

la salle de départ
departure lounge

les départs
departures

la destination
destination

les arrivées
arrivals

l'écran d'information
information screen

la boutique hors taxes
duty-free shop

le retrait des bagages
baggage reclaim

la station de taxis
taxi rank

la location de voitures
car hire

le navire • ship

le radar	l'antenne radio	le pont	la cheminée	le pont arrière
radar	radio antenna	deck	funnel	quarterdeck

la proue
prow

la marque de flottaison
Plimsoll line

le hublot
porthole

la coque
hull

le canot de sauvetage
lifeboat

la quille
keel

l'hélice
propeller

le paquebot
ocean liner

la passerelle de commandement
bridge

la salle des moteurs
engine room

la cabine
cabin

la cuisine
galley

vocabulaire • vocabulary

le dock	**le guindeau**
dock	windlass
le port	**le capitaine**
port	captain
la passerelle	**le runabout**
gangway	speedboat
l'ancre	**la barque**
anchor	rowing boat
le bollard	**le canoë**
bollard	canoe

autres bateaux · other ships

le ferry
ferry

le hors-bord
outboard motor

le canot pneumatique
inflatable dinghy

l'hydroptère
hydrofoil

le yacht
yacht

le catamaran
catamaran

le remorqueur
tug boat

l'aéroglisseur
hovercraft

le navire porte-conteneurs
container ship

le gréement
rigging

le voilier
sailboat

la cale
hold

le cargo
freighter

le pétrolier
oil tanker

le porte-avions
aircraft carrier

le navire de guerre
battleship

le kiosque
conning tower

le sous-marin
submarine

le port · port

l'entrepôt
warehouse

la grue
crane

le chariot élévateur
fork-lift truck

la route d'accès
access road

le bureau des
douanes
customs house

le dock
dock

le conteneur
container

le quai
quay

la cargaison
cargo

le terminal de ferrys
ferry terminal

le ferry
ferry

le guichet
ticket office

le
passager
passenger

le port de conteneurs | container port

le port de passagers | passenger port

le filet
net

le bateau de pêche
fishing boat

les amarres
mooring

la marina
marina

le port de pêche
fishing port

le port
harbour

l'embarcadère
pier

la jetée
jetty

le chantier naval
shipyard

le feu
lamp

le phare
lighthouse

la bouée
buoy

vocabulaire • vocabulary		
le garde-côte coastguard	**la cale sèche** dry dock	**embarquer** board (v)
le capitaine de port harbour master	**mouiller** moor (v)	**débarquer** disembark (v)
jeter l'ancre drop anchor (v)	**se mettre à quai** dock (v)	**prendre la mer** set sail (v)

les sports
sports

le football américain • American football

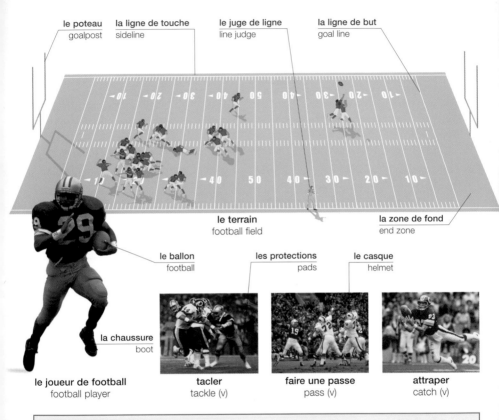

le poteau
goalpost

la ligne de touche
sideline

le juge de ligne
line judge

la ligne de but
goal line

le terrain
football field

la zone de fond
end zone

le ballon
football

les protections
pads

le casque
helmet

la chaussure
boot

le joueur de football
football player

tacler
tackle (v)

faire une passe
pass (v)

attraper
catch (v)

vocabulaire • vocabulary				
le temps mort time out	**l'équipe** team	**la défense** defence	**la majorette** cheerleader	**Où en est le match?** What is the score?
la prise de ballon maladroite fumble	**l'attaque** attack	**le score** score	**le but** touchdown	**Qui est-ce qui gagne?** Who is winning?

le rugby • rugby

le but
goal

la surface de but
in goal area

la ligne de touche
touch line

le drapeau
flag

la ligne de ballon
mort
dead ball line

le terrain de rugby | rugby pitch

le ballon
ball

lancer
throw (v)

le maillot de
rugby
rugby strip

botter
kick (v)

faire une passe
pass (v)

tacler
tackle (v)

l'essai
try

le joueur
player

la mêlée ouverte | ruck

la mêlée | scrum

le football • soccer

l'avant
forward

l'arbitre
referee

le cercle central
centre circle

le ballon
football

le gardien de but
goalkeeper

la tenue
football strip

le joueur de foot
footballer

le terrain
football pitch

le poteau
goalpost

le filet
net

la barre
transversale
crossbar

dribbler | dribble (v)

faire une tête
head (v)

le but | goal

le mur
wall

le coup franc | free kick

la surface de
réparation
penalty area

la ligne de but
goal line

la surface de but
goal area

le but
goal

le défenseur
defender

le juge de ligne
linesman

le drapeau de coin
corner flag

la rentrée en touche
throw-in

botter
kick (v)

la chaussure
boot

faire une passe
pass (v)

shooter
shoot (v)

sauver
save (v)

tacler
tackle (v)

vocabulaire • vocabulary				
le stade stadium	**la faute** foul	**le carton jaune** yellow card	**le championnat** league	**la prolongation** extra time
marquer un but score a goal (v)	**le corner** corner	**l'hors-jeu** off-side	**l'égalité** draw	**le remplaçant** substitute
le penalty penalty	**le carton rouge** red card	**l'expulsion** send off	**la mi-temps** half time	**le remplacement** substitution

le hockey • hockey

le hockey sur glace • ice hockey

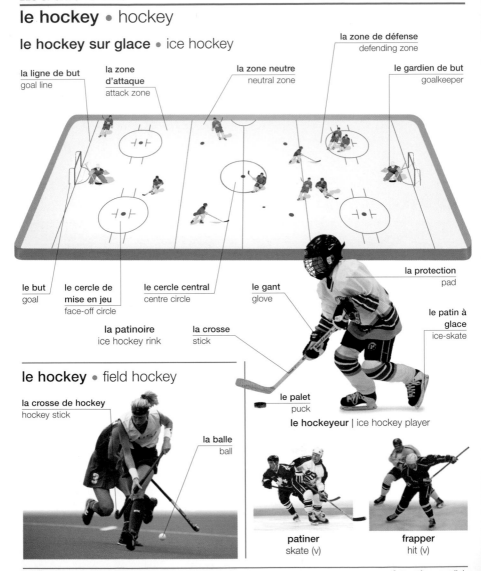

la zone de défense
defending zone

la ligne de but
goal line

la zone d'attaque
attack zone

la zone neutre
neutral zone

le gardien de but
goalkeeper

le but
goal

le cercle de mise en jeu
face-off circle

le cercle central
centre circle

le gant
glove

la protection
pad

le patin à glace
ice-skate

la patinoire
ice hockey rink

la crosse
stick

le hockey • field hockey

la crosse de hockey
hockey stick

la balle
ball

le palet
puck

le hockeyeur | ice hockey player

patiner
skate (v)

frapper
hit (v)

le cricket • cricket

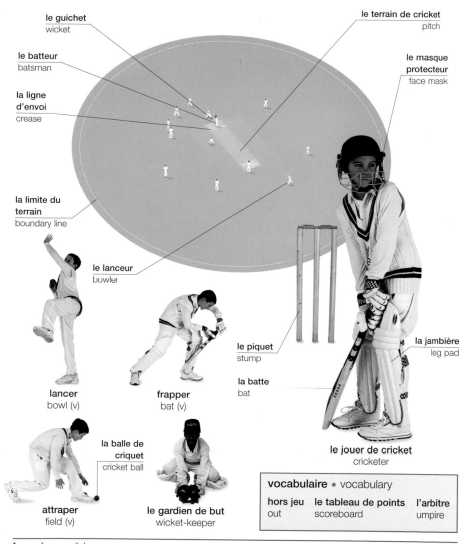

le guichet
wicket

le terrain de cricket
pitch

le batteur
batsman

le masque
protecteur
face mask

la ligne
d'envoi
crease

la limite du
terrain
boundary line

le lanceur
bowler

le piquet
stump

la jambière
leg pad

la batte
bat

lancer
bowl (v)

frapper
bat (v)

le jouer de cricket
cricketer

la balle de
criquet
cricket ball

attraper
field (v)

le gardien de but
wicket-keeper

vocabulaire • vocabulary		
hors jeu	**le tableau de points**	**l'arbitre**
out	scoreboard	umpire

le basket • basketball

la ligne de touche
sideline

l'arbitre
referee

le cercle central
centre circle

la ligne de lancer franc
free-throw line

la ligne de bout
endline

le terrain
court

la ligne de centre
centreline

la ligne de trois points
three-point line

le numéro
number

le panneau
backboard

le ballon
ball

l'anneau
hoop

le filet
net

le panier
basket

le joueur de basket | basketball player

vocabulaire • vocabulary

la passe pass	la rentrée throw-in
la faute foul	l'entre-deux jump ball
le rebond rebound	hors jeu out of bounds

les actions • actions

lancer
throw (v)

attraper
catch (v)

tirer
shoot (v)

sauter
jump (v)

marquer
mark (v)

bloquer
block (v)

faire rebondir
bounce (v)

faire un dunk
dunk (v)

le volley • volleyball

bloquer
block (v)

le filet
net

faire une manchette
dig (v)

l'arbitre
referee

la genouillère
knee support

le terrain | court

le baseball • baseball

le terrain • field

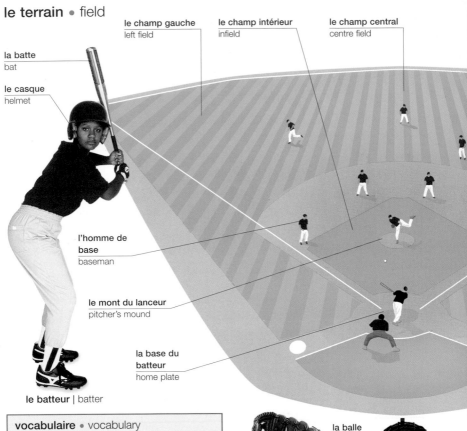

le champ gauche
left field

le champ intérieur
infield

le champ central
centre field

la batte
bat

le casque
helmet

l'homme de
base
baseman

le mont du lanceur
pitcher's mound

la base du
batteur
home plate

le batteur | batter

---

vocabulaire • vocabulary

le tour de batte inning	**sauf** safe	**la fausse balle** foul ball
le point run	**hors jeu** out	**le coup manqué** strike

la balle
ball

le gant
mitt

le masque
mask

---

le champ
extérieur
outfield

le champ droit
right field

la ligne de
pénalité
foul line

l'équipe
team

le banc de touche
dugout

le receveur
catcher

le lanceur
pitcher

les actions • actions

lancer | throw (v)

attraper | catch (v)

courir
run (v)

être en défense
field (v)

glisser
slide (v)

courser
tag (v)

lancer
pitch (v)

batter
bat (v)

l'arbitre
umpire

jouer | play (v)

le tennis • tennis

le manche
handle

la tête
head

la corde
string

l'arbitre
umpire

la ligne de fond
baseline

la raquette
racquet

la ligne de service
service line

la ligne de côté
sideline

la balle
ball

le poignet
wristband

le court de tennis | tennis court

vocabulaire • vocabulary					
le simple singles	**le set** set	**l'égalité** deuce	**la faute** fault	**le slice** slice	**l'effet** spin
le double doubles	**le match** match	**l'avantage** advantage	**l'as** ace	**l'échange** rally	**le juge de ligne** linesman
le jeu game	**le tiebreak** tiebreak	**zéro** love	**l'amorti** dropshot	**net!** let!	**le championnat** championship

les coups • strokes

le filet
net

le smash
smash

le ramasseur
de balles
ballboy

servir
serve (v)

les tennis
tennis shoes

le joueur
player

le service
serve

la vollée
volley

le retour
return

le lob
lob

le coup droit
forehand

le revers
backhand

les jeux de raquette • racquet games

le volant
shuttlecock

la raquette
bat

le badminton
badminton

le tennis de table
table tennis

le squash
squash

le racquetball
racquetball

le golf • golf

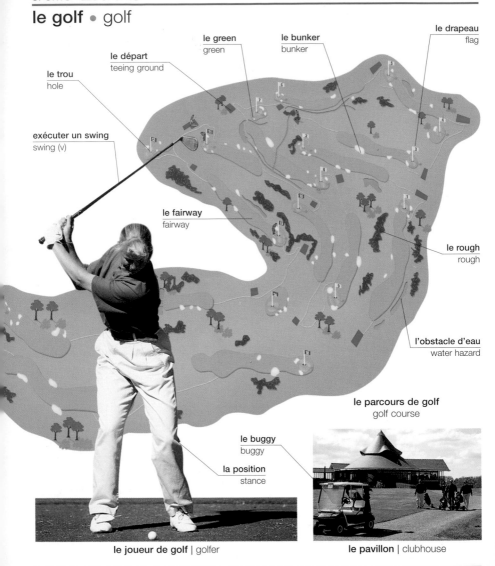

le green
green

le bunker
bunker

le drapeau
flag

le départ
teeing ground

le trou
hole

exécuter un swing
swing (v)

le fairway
fairway

le rough
rough

l'obstacle d'eau
water hazard

le parcours de golf
golf course

le buggy
buggy

la position
stance

le joueur de golf | golfer

le pavillon | clubhouse

l'équipement • equipment

la balle de golf
golf ball

le parapluie
umbrella

le sac de golf
golf bag

les pointes
spikes

le tee
tee

le gant
glove

le caddie
golf trolley

la chaussure de golf
golf shoe

les clubs de golf • golf clubs

le bois
wood

le putter
putter

le fer
iron

la cale
wedge

les actions • actions

partir du tee
tee off (v)

driver
drive (v)

putter
putt (v)

cocher
chip (v)

vocabulaire • vocabulary

le par par	**le over par** over par	**le handicap** handicap	**le caddie** caddy	**le swing en arrière** backswing	**le coup** stroke
le under par under par	**le trou en un** hole in one	**le tournoi** tournament	**les spectateurs** spectators	**le swing d'essai** practice swing	**la ligne de jeu** line of play

l'athlétisme • athletics

le couloir
lane

la piste
track

la ligne d'arrivée
finishing line

la ligne de départ
starting line

le terrain
field

l'athlète
athlete

le bloc de
départ
starting
blocks

le sprinter
sprinter

le disque
discus

le lancement du
poids
shotput

le javelot
javelin

vocabulaire • vocabulary

la course	le record	le photo-finish	le saut à la perche
race	record	photo finish	pole vault
le temps	battre un record	le marathon	le record personnel
time	break a record (v)	marathon	personal best

le chronomètre
stopwatch

le bâton
baton

le relais
relay race

la barre
crossbar

le saut en hauteur
high jump

le saut en longueur
long jump

les haies
hurdles

la gymnastique • gymnastics

le tremplin
springboard

le cheval
horse

le salto
somersault

le tapis
mat

le saut
vault

les exercises au sol
floor exercises

la gymnaste
gymnast

la poutre
beam

le drapeau
ribbon

la cabriole
tumble

la gymnastique rythmique
rhythmic gymnastics

---

vocabulaire • vocabulary

la barre fixe horizontal bar	**le cheval d'arçons** pommel horse	**les anneaux** rings	**les médailles** medals	**l'argent** silver
les barres parallèles parallel bars	**les barres asymétriques** asymmetric bars	**le podium** podium	**l'or** gold	**le bronze** bronze

les sports de combat • combat sports

l'adversaire
opponent

le protège-tête
guard

le gant
glove

la ceinture
belt

le karaté
karate

le taekwondo
tae-kwon-do

le masque
mask

le judo
judo

le sabre
sword

l'aïkido
aikido

le kendo
kendo

le kung-fu
kung fu

la boxe thaïlandaise
kickboxing

la lutte
wrestling

la boxe
boxing

les actions • actions

la chute
fall

la prise
hold

la projection
throw

l'immobilisation
pin

le coup de pied
kick

le coup de poing
punch

le coup
strike

le saut
jump

le blocage
block

le coup
chop

vocabulaire • vocabulary

le ring boxing ring	**le round** round	**le poing** fist	**la ceinture noire** black belt	**la capoeira** capoeira
les gants de boxe boxing gloves	**le combat** bout	**le knock-out** knock out	**l'autodéfense** self defence	**le sumo** sumo wrestling
le protège-dents mouth guard	**l'entraînement** sparring	**le punching-bag** punch bag	**les arts martiaux** martial arts	**le taï chi** tai-chi

la natation • swimming
l'équipement • equipment

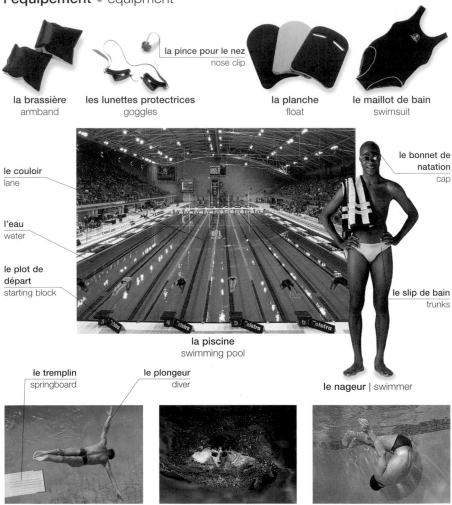

la pince pour le nez
nose clip

la brassière
armband

les lunettes protectrices
goggles

la planche
float

le maillot de bain
swimsuit

le couloir
lane

le bonnet de natation
cap

l'eau
water

le plot de départ
starting block

le slip de bain
trunks

la piscine
swimming pool

le nageur | swimmer

le tremplin
springboard

le plongeur
diver

plonger | dive (v)

nager | swim (v)

le tour | turn

les styles • styles

le crawl
front crawl

la brasse
breaststroke

la nage
stroke

le coup de pied
kick

le dos crawlé | backstroke

le papillon | butterfly

la plongée • scuba diving

la bouteille d'air
air cylinder

la combinaison de plongée
wetsuit

le tuba
snorkel

le masque
mask

la palme
flipper

la ceinture de plomb
weight belt

le régulateur
regulator

vocabulaire • vocabulary

le plongeon dive	**nager sur place** tread water (v)	**les casiers** lockers	**le water-polo** water polo	**le petit bassin** shallow end	**la crampe** cramp
le plongeon de haut vol high dive	**le départ plongé** racing dive	**le maître nageur** lifeguard	**le grand bassin** deep end	**la nage synchronisée** synchronized swimming	**se noyer** drown (v)

la voile • sailing

le compas
compass

l'ancre
anchor

le mât
mast

le gréement
rigging

la grand-voile
mainsail

la voile d'avant
headsail

le taquet
cleat

le pont de côté
sidedeck

la bôme
boom

l'avant
bow

l'arrière
stern

la barre
tiller

la coque
hull

naviguer | navigate (v)

le yacht | yacht

la sécurité • safety

la fusée éclairante
flare

la bouée de sauvetage
lifebuoy

le gilet de sauvetage
life jacket

le radeau de sauvetage
life raft

les sports aquatiques • watersports

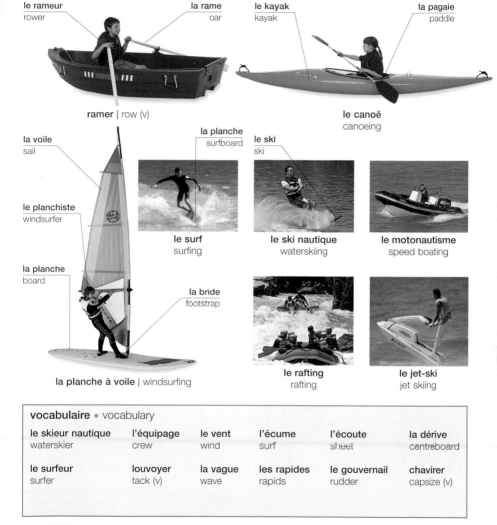

le rameur
rower

la rame
oar

le kayak
kayak

la pagaie
paddle

ramer | row (v)

le canoë
canoeing

la voile
sail

la planche
surfboard

le ski
ski

le planchiste
windsurfer

la planche
board

la bride
footstrap

le surf
surfing

le ski nautique
waterskiing

le motonautisme
speed boating

la planche à voile | windsurfing

le rafting
rafting

le jet-ski
jet skiing

---

vocabulaire • vocabulary

le skieur nautique waterskier	**l'équipage** crew	**le vent** wind	**l'écume** surf	**l'écoute** sheet	**la dérive** centreboard
le surfeur surfer	**louvoyer** tack (v)	**la vague** wave	**les rapides** rapids	**le gouvernail** rudder	**chavirer** capsize (v)

---

l'équitation • horse riding

la bombe
riding hat

la crinière
mane

le cavalier
rider

les rênes
reins

la selle
saddle

le cheval
horse

le jodhpur
jodhpurs

la queue
tail

la sangle
girth

la botte
riding boot

l'étrier
stirrup

le sabot
hoof

le pommeau
pommel

le frontail
browband

la muserolle
noseband

le mors
bit

le siège
seat

le fer à cheval
horseshoe

la selle de femme
side-saddle

la bride | bridle

la cravache | riding crop

les courses • events

le cheval de course
racehorse

la course de chevaux
horse race

l'obstacle
fence

le steeple
steeplechase

la course de trot
harness race

le rodéo
rodeo

le jumping
showjumping

la course attelée
carriage race

la randonnée
trekking

le dressage
dressage

le polo
polo

vocabulaire • vocabulary

le pas walk	**le petit galop** canter	**le saut** jump	**le licou** halter	**l'enclos** paddock	**la course de plat** flat race
le trot trot	**le galop** gallop	**le valet d'écurie** groom	**l'écurie** stable	**l'arène** arena	**le champs de courses** racecourse

la pêche • fishing

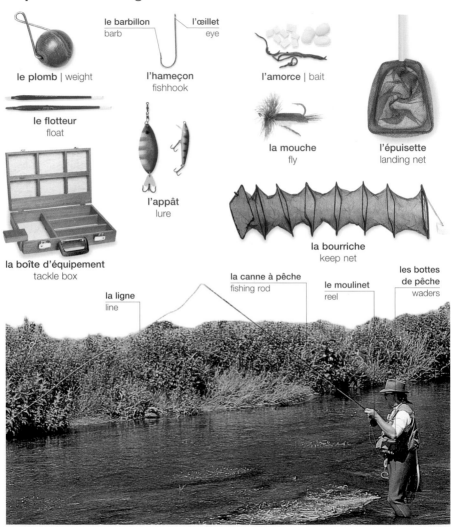

le plomb | weight

le flotteur
float

la boîte d'équipement
tackle box

le barbillon
barb

l'œillet
eye

l'hameçon
fishhook

l'appât
lure

l'amorce | bait

la mouche
fly

l'épuisette
landing net

la bourriche
keep net

la ligne
line

la canne à pêche
fishing rod

le moulinet
reel

**les bottes
de pêche**
waders

le pêcheur | angler

les genres de pêche • types of fishing

la pêche en eau douce
freshwater fishing

la pêche à la mouche
fly fishing

la pêche sportive
sport fishing

la pêche hauturière
deep sea fishing

**la pêche au lancer
en mer**
surfcasting

---

les activités • activities

lancer
cast (v)

attraper
catch (v)

ramener
reel in (v)

prendre au filet
net (v)

lâcher
release (v)

---

vocabulaire • vocabulary

amorcer bait (v)	**le matériel de pêche** tackle	**l'imperméable** waterproofs	**le permis de pêche** fishing permit	**le panier de pêche** creel
mordre bite (v)	**le tambour** spool	**la perche** pole	**la pêche maritime** marine fishing	**la pêche sous-marine** spearfishing

le ski • skiing

la pente de ski
ski slope

le télésiège
chairlift

la télécabine
cable car

la combinaison
de ski
ski suit

le bâton de
ski
ski pole

le gant
glove

la piste de ski
ski run

la chaussure de ski
ski boot

la barrière de sécurité
safety barrier

le ski
ski

la carre
edge

la skieuse
skier

la pointe
tip

les épreuves • events

la descente
downhill skiing

la porte
gate

le slalom
slalom

le saut
ski jump

le ski de randonnée
cross-country skiing

les sports d'hiver • winter sports

l'escalade en glace
ice climbing

le patinage
ice-skating

le patinage artistique
figure skating

les lunettes de ski
goggles

le patin à glace
skate

le surf des neiges
snowboarding

le bobsleigh
bobsleigh

la luge
luge

l'autoneige
snowmobile

la luge
sledding

vocabulaire • vocabulary

le ski alpin alpine skiing	**le traîneau à chiens** dog sledding
le slalom géant giant slalom	**le patinage de vitesse** speed skating
hors piste off-piste	**le biathlon** biathlon
le curling curling	**l'avalanche** avalanche

les autres sports • other sports

le planeur
glider

le deltaplane
hang-glider

le vol plané
gliding

le parachute
parachute

le deltaplane
hang-gliding

la corde
rope

l'escalade
rock climbing

le parachutisme
parachuting

le parapente
paragliding

le saut en chute libre
skydiving

le rappel
abseiling

le saut à l'élastique
bungee jumping

le rallye
rally driving

le coureur
automobile
racing driver

la course automobile
motor racing

le motocross
motorcross

la course de moto
motorbike racing

la planche à
roulettes
skateboard

le patin à
roulettes
rollerskate

**la planche à
roulettes**
skateboarding

le patinage à roulettes
roller skating

la crosse
stick

le lacrosse
lacrosse

le
masque
mask

le
fleuret
foil

l'escrime
fencing

la quille
pin

l'arc
bow

la cible
target

la flèche
arrow

le carquois
quiver

le tir à l'arcx
archery

le tir à cible
target shooting

la boule de
bowling
bowling ball

le bowling
bowling

le billard américain
pool

le billard
snooker

le conditionnement physique • fitness

**le vélo
d'entraînement**
exercise bike

l'appareil de gym
gym machine

le banc
bench

les poids
free weights

la barre
bar

le gymnase
gym

la machine à ramer
rowing machine

**l'escalier
d'entraînement**
step machine

la tapis roulant
treadmill

**la machine de
randonnée**
cross trainer

**l'entraîneuse
individuelle**
personal trainer

la piscine
swimming pool

le sauna
sauna

les exercices • exercises

l'étirement
stretch

la fente en avant
lunge

le collant
tights

la traction
press-up

le redressement
assis
sit-up

l'exercise pour
les biceps
bicep curl

l'haltère
dumb bell

la traction pour les
jambes
leg press

la flexion de jambes
squat

l'exercice pour la
poitrine
chest press

les
baskets
trainers

la barre à
poids
weight bar

l'entraînement poids
et haltères
weight training

le maillot
vest

le jogging
jogging

l'aérobic
aerobics

vocabulaire • vocabulary

s'entraîner train (v)	jogger sur place jog on the spot (v)	étendre extend (v)	les exercices Pilates Pilates	l'entraînement en circuit circuit training
s'échauffer warm up (v)	fléchir flex (v)	tirer pull up (v)	l'aéroboxe boxercise	le saut à la corde skipping

le temps libre
leisure

le théâtre • theatre

le rideau
curtain

les coulisses
wings

le décor
set

le public
audience

l'orchestre
orchestra

la scène | stage

le fauteuil
seat

la deuxième galerie
upper circle

la rangée
row

la loge
box

la corbeille
circle

le balcon
balcony

l'allée
aisle

l'orchestre
stalls

les places | seating

vocabulaire • vocabulary

la distribution cast	**le texte** script	**la première** first night
l'acteur actor	**la toile de fond** backdrop	**l'entracte** interval
l'actrice actress	**le metteur en scène** director	**le programme** programme
la pièce de théâtre play	**le metteur en scène** producer	**la fosse d'orchestre** orchestra pit

le concert
concert

la comédie musicale
musical

le costume
costume

le ballet
ballet

l'opéra
opera

vocabulaire • vocabulary

le placeur usher	**la bande sonore** soundtrack	**Ça commence à quelle heure?** What time does it start?
la musique classique classical music	**applaudir** applaud (v)	**Je voudrais deux billets pour la représentation de ce soir.** I'd like two tickets for tonight's performance.
la partition musical score	**le bis** encore	

le cinéma • cinema

le pop-corn
popcorn

le foyer
lobby

la caisse
box office

l'affiche
poster

la salle de cinéma
cinema hall

l'écran
screen

vocabulaire • vocabulary

la comédie comedy	**la comédie romantique** romance
le thriller thriller	**le film de science-fiction** science fiction film
le film d'horreur horror film	**le film d'aventures** adventure
le western western	**le film d'animation** animated film

l'orchestre • orchestra

les cordes • strings

la harpe harp	**le chef d'orchestre** conductor	**le contrebasse** double bass

le violon violin	**le podium** podium	**l'alto** viola	**le violoncelle** cello

la partition score

la clé de sol treble clef

la note note

la portée staff

la clé de fa bass clef

le piano | piano

la notation | notation

vocabulaire • vocabulary

l'ouverture overture	**la sonate** sonata	**le silence** rest	**le dièse** sharp	**le bécarre** natural	**la gamme** scale
la symphonie symphony	**les instruments** instruments	**le ton** pitch	**le bémol** flat	**la barre de mesure** bar	**la baguette** baton

les bois • woodwind

le piccolo
piccolo

la flûte traversière
flute

le hautbois
oboe

le cor anglais
cor anglais

la clarinette
clarinet

la clarinette
bass clarinet

le basson
bassoon

le contrebasson
double bassoon

le saxophone
saxophone

la percussion • percussion

les bongos
bongos

la caisse claire
snare drum

la timbale
kettledrum

le gong
gong

les cymbales
cymbals

le tambour
tambourine

le triangle
triangle

les maracas
maracas

le vibraphone
vibraphone

les cuivres • brass

la trompette
trumpet

le trombone
trombone

le cor
French horn

le tuba
tuba

le concert • concert

le chanteur
lead singer

le microphone
microphone

le batteur
drummer

le guitariste
guitarist

les fans
fans

le haut-parleur
speaker

le bassiste
bass guitarist

le concert de rock | rock concert

les instruments • instruments

le pick-up
pickup

le manche
neck

le sillet
fret

la cheville
tuning peg

la corde
string

le chevalet
bridge

le tambour
drum

la basse
bass guitar

le piano électronique
keyboard

la guitare électrique
electric guitar

la batterie
drum kit

les styles de musique • musical styles

le jazz
jazz

le blues
blues

la musique punk
punk

la musique folk
folk music

la pop
pop

la dance
dance

le rap
rap

la heavy métal
heavy metal

la musique classique
classical music

vocabulaire • vocabulary						
la chanson	**les paroles**	**la mélodie**	**le beat**	**le reggae**	**la country**	**le projecteur**
song	lyrics	melody	beat	reggae	country	spotlight

le tourisme • sightseeing

l'attraction touristique | tourist attraction

le touriste
tourist

l'itinéraire
itinerary

à impériale
open-top

le bus touristique | tour bus

la guide
tour guide

la statuette
statuette

la visite guidée
guided tour

les souvenirs
souvenirs

---

vocabulaire • vocabulary

ouvert open	**le guide** guide book	**le caméscope** camcorder	**à gauche** left	**Où est…?** Where is…?
fermé closed	**la pellicule** film	**l'appareil photo** camera	**à droite** right	**Je me suis perdu.** I'm lost.
le prix d'entrée entrance fee	**les piles** batteries	**les directions** directions	**tout droit** straight on	**Pour aller à…, s'il vous plaît?** Can you tell me the way to….?

les attractions • attractions

le tableau
painting

l'objet exposé
exhibit

l'exposition
exhibition

la ruine célèbre
famous ruin

le musée d'art
art gallery

le monument
monument

le musée
museum

**le monument
historique**
historic building

le casino
casino

le parc
gardens

le parc national
national park

l'information • information

les heures
times

le plan
floor plan

le plan
map

l'horaire
timetable

**l'information
touristique**
tourist information

---

les activités de plein air • outdoor activities

le sentier
footpath

le cadran solaire
sundial

le café
café

le parc | park

la pelouse
grass

le banc
bench

les jardins à la française
formal gardens

les montagnes russes
roller coaster

la foire
fairground

le parc d'attractions
theme park

la réserve
safari park

le zoo
zoo

les activités • activites

le vélo
cycling

le jogging
jogging

la planche à roulette
skateboarding

le roller
rollerblading

la piste cavalière
bridle path

l'observation des oiseaux
bird watching

l'équitation
horse riding

la randonnée
hiking

le panier à pique-nique
hamper

le pique-nique
picnic

le terrain de jeux • playground

le bac à sable
sandpit

la pataugeoire
paddling pool

la balançoire
swings

la bascule | seesaw

le toboggan
slide

la cage à poules
climbing frame

la plage • beach

l'hôtel
hotel

le parasol
beach umbrella

la cabine de plage
beach hut

le sable
sand

la vague
wave

la mer
sea

le sac de plage
beach bag

le bikini
bikini

prendre un bain de soleil | sunbathe (v)

la tour de surveillance
lifeguard tower

le maître nageur
lifeguard

le pare-vent
windbreak

la promenade
promenade

le transat
deck chair

les lunettes de soleil
sunglasses

le chapeau de plage
sunhat

la lotion solaire
suntan lotion

l'écran total
sunblock

le ballon de plage
beach ball

la bouée
rubber ring

la serviette de plage
beach towel

le maillot de bain
swimsuit

la pelle
spade

le seau
bucket

le château de sable
sandcastle

le coquillage
shell

le camping • camping

les toilettes
toilets

les poubelles
waste disposal

les douches
shower block

le branchement électrique
electric hook-up

le double toit
flysheet

le piquet
tent peg

la corde
guy rope

la caravane
caravan

le terrain de camping
campsite

---

vocabulaire • vocabulary

camper camp (v)	**l'emplacement** pitch	**le banc à pique-nique** picnic bench	**le charbon de bois** charcoal
le bureau du chef site manager's office	**monter une tente** pitch a tent (v)	**le hamac** hammock	**l'allume-feu** firelighter
les emplacements libres pitches available	**le mât** tent pole	**le camping-car** camper van	**allumer un feu** light a fire (v)
complet full	**le lit de camp** camp bed	**la remorque** trailer	**le feu de camp** campfire

---

le cadre
frame

le tapis de sol
ground sheet

le sac à dos
backpack

le thermos
vacuum flask

la bouteille d'eau
water bottle

la tente
tent

la moustiquaire
mosquito net

le spray contre les
insects
insect repellent

la lampe torche
torch

les sous-vêtements
thermiques
thermals

les chaussures de
marche
walking boots

l'imperméable
waterproofs

le sac de couchage
sleeping bag

le tapis de sol
sleeping mat

le réchaud
camping stove

le barbecue
barbecue

le matelat pneumatique | air mattress

les distractions à la maison • home entertainment

le DVD
DVD disk

le baladeur CD
personal CD player

l'enregistreur minidisk
mini disk recorder

le baladeur MP3
MP3 player

le lecteur DVD
DVD player

le tourne-disque
record player

le lecteur CD
CD player

le baffle
(loud) speaker

la radio
radio

l'amplificateur
amplifier

les écouteurs
headphones

le support
speaker stand

l'étagère
stand

la chaîne hi-fi
hi-fi system

la vidéocassette
video tape

l'écran
screen

l'œilleton
eyecup

le magnétoscope
video recorder

le caméscope
camcorder

l'antenne parabolique
satellite dish

la télévision 16/9ème
widescreen television

la console
console

l'avance rapide
fast forward

la pause
pause

l'enregistrement
record

le volume
volume

la commande
controller

le retour rapide
rewind

l'arrêt
stop

la lecture
play

le jeu vidéo | video game

la télécommande
remote control

---

vocabulaire • vocabulary

le CD compact disc	**le film** feature film	**le programme** programme	**la chaîne à péage** pay per view channel	**regarder la télévision** watch television (v)
la cassette cassette tape	**la publicité** advertisement	**stéréo** stereo	**changer de chaîne** change channel (v)	**éteindre la télévision** turn the television off (v)
le lecteur cassettes cassette player	**numérique** digital	**la télévision par câble** cable television	**allumer la télévision** turn the television on (v)	**régler la radio** tune the radio (v)

---

la **photographie** • photography

le compteur de vues
frame counter

le flash
flash

le réglage de
l'ouverture
aperture dial

le filtre
filter

le déclencheur
shutter release

le bouchon d'objectif
lens caps

le réglage du temps de
pose
shutter-speed dial

l'objectif
lens

l'appareil réflex mono-objectif | SLR camera

le flash compact
flash gun

le posemètre
lightmeter

le zoom
zoom lens

le trépied
tripod

les **types d'appareils photo** • types of camera

l'appareil numérique
digital camera

l'appareil photo APS
APS camera

l'appareil instantané
instant camera

l'appareil jetable
disposable camera

photographier • photograph (v)

le rouleau
de pellicule
film spool

la pellicule
film

mettre au point
focus (v)

développer
develop (v)

le négatif
negative

paysage
landscape

portrait
portrait

la photo | photograph

l'album de photos
photo album

le cadre de photo
photo frame

les problèmes • problems

sous-exposé
underexposed

surexposé
overexposed

flou
out of focus

la tache rouge
red eye

---

vocabulaire • vocabulary

le viseur viewfinder	l'épreuve print
le sac d'appareil photo camera case	mat mat
la pose exposure	brilliant gloss
la chambre noire darkroom	l'agrandissement enlargement

Pourriez-vous faire développer cette pellicule?
I'd like this film processed

---

les jeux • games

l'échiquier
chessboard

noir
black

blanc
white

la dame
queen

le roi
king

le fou
bishop

le pion
pawn

la tour
rook

le cavalier
knight

les échecs
chess

la case
square

le pion
piece

la pièce
tile

les dames
draughts

le scrabble
scrabble

le dé
dice

le jeton
counter

le
monopoly
monopoly

le trictrac | backgammon

les jeux de société | board games

la philatélie
stamp collecting

le puzzle
jigsaw puzzle

les dominos
dominoes

la cible
dartboard

le mille
bullseye

les fléchettes
darts

le joker
joker

le valet
jack

la dame
queen

le roi
king

l'as
ace

le carreau
diamond

le pique
spade

le cœur
heart

le trèfle
club

les cartes
cards

battre | shuffle (v)

donner | deal (v)

---

vocabulaire • vocabulary

le coup move	**gagner** win (v)	**le perdant** loser	**le point** point	**le bridge** bridge	**Jette le dé.** Roll the dice.
jouer play (v)	**le gagnant** winner	**le jeu** game	**la marque** score	**le jeu de cartes** pack of cards	**C'est à qui de jouer?** Whose turn is it?
le joueur player	**perdre** lose (v)	**le pari** bet	**le poker** poker	**la couleur** suit	**C'est à toi de jouer.** It's your move.

les arts et métiers 1 • arts and crafts 1

l'artiste peintre
artist

le tableau
painting

le chevalet
easel

la toile
canvas

le pinceau
brush

la palette
palette

la peinture | painting

les couleurs • paints

les peintures à l'huile
oil paints

l'aquarelle
watercolour paint

les pastels
pastels

l'acrylique
acrylic paint

la gouache
poster paint

les couleurs • colours

rouge red	bleu blue	jaune yellow	vert green
orange orange	violet purple	blanc white	noir black
gris grey	rose pink	marron brown	indigo indigo

les autres arts • other crafts

le carnet à croquis
sketch pad

le croquis
sketch

l'encre
ink

le crayon
pencil

le fusain
charcoal

le dessin | drawing

l'imprimerie
printing

la gravure
engraving

la pierre
stone

le maillet
mallet

le burin
chisel

le bois
wood

la spatule
modelling tool

la sculpture
sculpting

la sculpture sur bois
woodworking

le tour de potier
potter's wheel

la colle
glue

le carton
cardboard

l'argile
clay

le collage | collage

la poterie
pottery

la joaillerie
jewellery making

le papier mâché
papier-mâché

l'origami
origami

le modélisme
model making

les arts et métiers 2 • arts and crafts 2

le guide de fil
thread guide

la bobine de fil
thread reel

l'aiguille
needle

le balancier
balance wheel

le pied-de-biche
presser foot

le sélecteur de point
stitch selector

la platine
needle plate

la machine à coudre | sewing machine

les ciseaux
scissors

le patron
pattern

la pelote à épingles
pincushion

l'épingle
pin

le centimètre
tape measure

le tissu
material

la corbeille à couture | sewing basket

le fil
thread

l'œillet
eye

la bobine
bobbin

l'agrafe
hook

le dé à coudre
thimble

la craie de tailleur
tailor's chalk

le mannequin
tailor's dummy

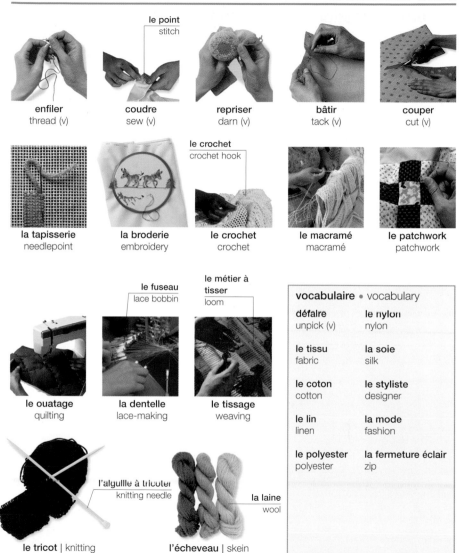

enfiler
thread (v)

coudre
sew (v)

le point
stitch

repriser
darn (v)

bâtir
tack (v)

couper
cut (v)

la tapisserie
needlepoint

la broderie
embroidery

le crochet
crochet hook

le crochet
crochet

le macramé
macramé

le patchwork
patchwork

le fuseau
lace bobbin

le métier à
tisser
loom

le ouatage
quilting

la dentelle
lace-making

le tissage
weaving

l'aiguille à tricoter
knitting needle

la laine
wool

le tricot | knitting

l'écheveau | skein

vocabulaire · vocabulary

défaire
unpick (v)

le nylon
nylon

le tissu
fabric

la soie
silk

le coton
cotton

le styliste
designer

le lin
linen

la mode
fashion

le polyester
polyester

la fermeture éclair
zip

l'environnement
environment

l'espace • space

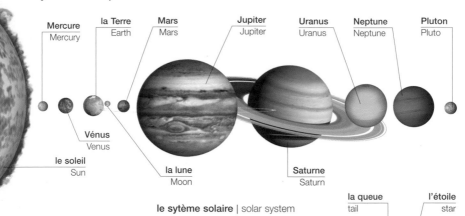

Mercure
Mercury

la Terre
Earth

Mars
Mars

Jupiter
Jupiter

Uranus
Uranus

Neptune
Neptune

Pluton
Pluto

Vénus
Venus

le soleil
Sun

la lune
Moon

Saturne
Saturn

le sytème solaire | solar system

la queue
tail

l'étoile
star

la galaxie
galaxy

la nébuleuse
nebula

l'astéroïde
asteroid

la comète
comet

vocabulaire • vocabulary

l'univers universe	**le trou noir** black hole	**la pleine lune** full moon
l'orbite orbit	**la planète** planet	**la nouvelle lune** new moon
la pesanteur gravity	**le météore** meteor	**le croissant de lune** crescent moon

l'éclipse | eclipse

l'exploration spatiale • space exploration

la navette spatiale
space shuttle

la fusée d'orientation
thruster

le radar
radar

le scaphandre spatial
space suit

le sas d'équipage
crew hatch

l'accélérateur
booster

l'astronaute | astronaut

le module lunaire | lunar module

la rampe de lancement
launch pad

le lancement
launch

le satellite
satellite

la station spatiale
space station

l'astronomie • astronomy

la constellation
constellation

les jumelles
binoculars

le télescope
telescope

le trépied
tripod

la terre • Earth

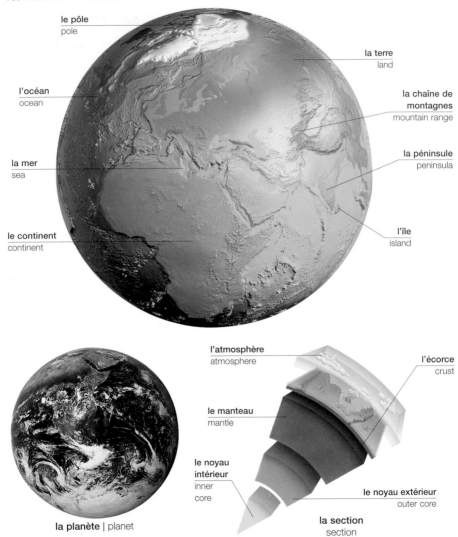

le pôle
pole

la terre
land

l'océan
ocean

la chaîne de
montagnes
mountain range

la mer
sea

la péninsule
peninsula

le continent
continent

l'île
island

l'atmosphère
atmosphere

l'écorce
crust

le manteau
mantle

le noyau
intérieur
inner
core

le noyau extérieur
outer core

la planète | planet

la section
section

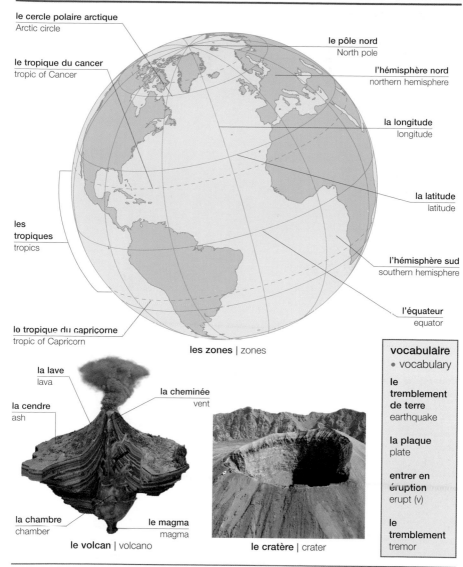

le cercle polaire arctique
Arctic circle

le tropique du cancer
tropic of Cancer

les tropiques
tropics

lo tropique du capricorne
tropic of Capricorn

le pôle nord
North pole

l'hémisphère nord
northern hemisphere

la longitude
longitude

la latitude
latitude

l'hémisphère sud
southern hemisphere

l'équateur
equator

les zones | zones

la lave
lava

la cheminée
vent

la cendre
ash

la chambre
chamber

le magma
magma

le volcan | volcano

le cratère | crater

vocabulaire
• vocabulary

le tremblement de terre
earthquake

la plaque
plate

entrer en éruption
erupt (v)

le tremblement
tremor

le paysage • landscape

la montagne
mountain

la pente
slope

la rive
bank

la rivière
river

les rapides
rapids

les rochers
rocks

le glacier
glacier

la vallée | valley

la colline
hill

le plateau
plateau

la gorge
gorge

la caverne
cave

la plaine | plain

le désert | desert

la forêt | forest

le bois | wood

la forêt tropicale
rainforest

le marais
swamp

le pré
meadow

la prairie
grassland

la cascade
waterfall

le ruisseau
stream

le lac
lake

le geyser
geyser

la côte
coast

la falaise
cliff

le récif de corail
coral reef

l'estuaire
estuary

le temps • weather

l'exosphère
exosphere

l'aurore
aurora

la thermosphère
thermosphere

la mésosphère
mesosphere

l'ionosphère
ionosphere

les rayons
ultraviolets
ultraviolet rays

la stratosphère
stratosphere

la couche d'ozone
ozone layer

la troposphère
troposphere

l'atmosphère | atmosphere

le soleil
sunshine

le vent
wind

---

vocabulaire • vocabulary

la neige fondue sleet	**l'averse** shower	**(très) chaud** hot	**sec** dry	**venteux** windy	**J'ai chaud/froid.** I'm hot/cold.
la grêle hail	**ensoleillé** sunny	**froid** cold	**humide** wet	**la tempête** gale	**Il pleut.** It's raining.
le tonnerre thunder	**nuageux** cloudy	**chaud** warm	**lourd** humid	**la température** temperature	**Il fait … degrés.** It's … degrees.

le nuage
cloud

la pluie
rain

l'éclair
lightning

l'orage
storm

la brume
mist

le brouillard
fog

l'arc-en-ciel
rainbow

la neige
snow

le givre
frost

le glaçon
icicle

la glace
ice

le gel
freeze

l'ouragan
hurricane

la tornade
tornado

la mousson
monsoon

l'inondation
flood

les roches • rocks

igné • igneous

le granit
granite

l'obsidienne
obsidian

le basalte
basalt

la pierre ponce
pumice

sédimentaire • sedimentary

le grès
sandstone

le calcaire
limestone

la craie
chalk

le silex
flint

le conglomérat
conglomerate

le charbon
coal

métamorphique • metamorphic

l'ardoise
slate

le schiste
schist

le gneiss
gneiss

le marbre
marble

les gemmes • gems

le rubis
ruby

l'aigue-marine
aquamarine

l'améthyste
amethyst

le diamant
diamond

le jade
jade

le jais
jet

l'émeraude
emerald

l'opale
opal

le saphir
sapphire

la pierre de lune
moonstone

le grenat
garnet

le topaze
topaz

la toumaline
tourmaline

les minéraux • minerals

le quartz
quartz

le mica
mica

le soufre
sulphur

l'hématite
hematite

la calcite
calcite

la malachite
malachite

la turquoise
turquoise

l'onyx
onyx

l'agate
agate

le graphite
graphite

les métaux • metals

l'or
gold

l'argent
silver

le platine
platinum

le nickel
nickel

le fer
iron

le cuivre
copper

l'étain
tin

l'aluminium
aluminium

le mercure
mercury

le zinc
zinc

les animaux 1 • animals 1
les mammifères • mammals

les poils
whiskers

la queue
tail

le lapin
rabbit

le hamster
hamster

la souris
mouse

le rat
rat

le hérisson
hedgehog

l'écureuil
squirrel

la chauve-souris
bat

le raton laveur
raccoon

le renard
fox

le loup
wolf

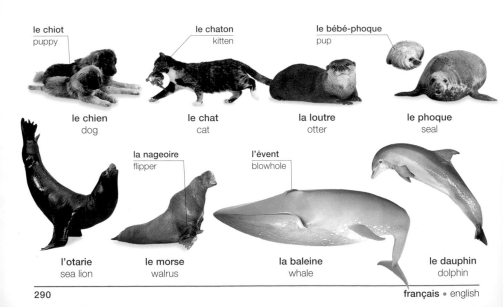

le chiot
puppy

le chaton
kitten

le bébé-phoque
pup

le chien
dog

le chat
cat

la loutre
otter

le phoque
seal

la nageoire
flipper

l'évent
blowhole

l'otarie
sea lion

le morse
walrus

la baleine
whale

le dauphin
dolphin

la ramure
antler

la crinière
mane

le sabot
hoof

la bosse
hump

le cerf
deer

le zèbre
zebra

la girafe
giraffe

le chameau
camel

la trompe
trunk

la défense
tusk

la corne
horn

l'hippopotame
hippopotamus

l'éléphant
elephant

le rhinocéros
rhinoceros

le tigre
tiger

la crinière
mane

le lion
lion

le singe
monkey

le gorille
gorilla

le koala
koala

la poche
pouch

le panda
panda

la griffe
claw

le kangourou
kangaroo

l'ours
bear

l'ours blanc
polar bear

les animaux 2 • animals 2
les oiseaux • birds

la queue
tail

le canari
canary

le moineau
sparrow

le colibri
hummingbird

l'hirondelle
swallow

le corbeau
crow

le pigeon
pigeon

le pic
woodpecker

le faucon
falcon

la chouette
owl

la mouette
gull

l'aigle
eagle

le pélican
pelican

le flamant
flamingo

la cigogne
stork

la grue
crane

le pingouin
penguin

l'autruche
ostrich

l'oie | goose

le cygne
swan

les reptiles • reptiles

les écailles
scales

l'alligator
alligator

le paon
peacock

le faisan
pheasant

le lézard
lizard

l'iguane
iguana

le dindon
turkey

la carapace
shell

la tortue marine
turtle

la tortue
tortoise

le bec
bill

la plume
feather

l'aile
wing

le serpent
snake

le museau
snout

le cacatoès
cockatoo

la griffe
claw

le perroquet
parrot

le crocodile
crocodile

les animaux 3 • animals 3
les amphibiens • amphibians

la grenouille frog	**le crapaud** toad	**le têtard** tadpole	**la salamandre** salamander

les poissons • fish

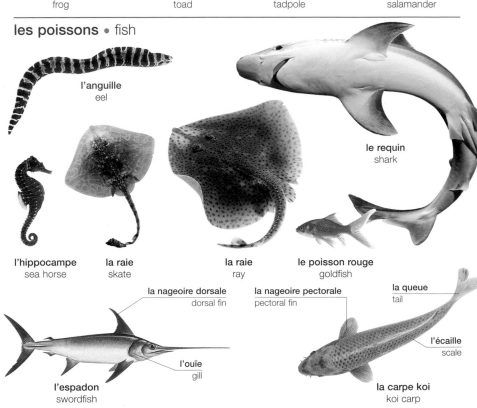

l'anguille
eel

le requin
shark

l'hippocampe
sea horse

la raie
skate

la raie
ray

le poisson rouge
goldfish

la nageoire dorsale
dorsal fin

la nageoire pectorale
pectoral fin

la queue
tail

l'écaille
scale

l'ouïe
gill

l'espadon
swordfish

la carpe koi
koi carp

les invertébrés • invertebrates

la fourmi
ant

la termite
termite

l'abeille
bee

la guêpe
wasp

le scarabée
beetle

le cafard
cockroach

le papillon
moth

l'antenne
antenna

le papillon
butterfly

le cocon
cocoon

la chenille
caterpillar

le grillon
cricket

la sauterelle
grasshopper

la mante religieuse
praying mantis

le dard
sting

le scorpion
scorpion

le mille-pattes
centipede

la libellule
dragonfly

la mouche
fly

le moustique
mosquito

la coccinelle
ladybird

l'araignée
spider

la limace
slug

l'escargot
snail

le ver
worm

l'étoile de mer
starfish

la moule
mussel

le crabe
crab

le homard
lobster

la pieuvre
octopus

le calmar
squid

la méduse
jellyfish

les plantes • plants

l'arbre • tree

la branche
branch

la feuille
leaf

la brindille
twig

l'écorce
bark

le saule
willow

la racine
root

le tronc
trunk

le chêne
oak

le peuplier
poplar

l'eucalyptus
eucalyptus

le mélèze
larch

le hêtre
beech

le bouleau
birch

le pin
pine

le cèdre
cedar

l'érable
maple

l'orme
elm

le tilleul
lime

le houx
holly

la baie
berry

le palmier
palm

la plante à fleurs • flowering plant

la fleur
flower

l'étamine
stamen

le pétale
petal

le calice
calyx

la tige
stalk

la tige
stem

le bouton
bud

la renoncule
buttercup

la pâquerette
daisy

le chardon
thistle

le pissenlit
dandelion

la bruyère
heather

le coquelicot
poppy

la digitale
foxglove

le chèvrefeuille
honeysuckle

le tournesol
sunflower

le trèfle
clover

**les jacinthes
des bois**
bluebells

la primevère
primrose

les lupins
lupins

l'ortie
nettle

la ville • town

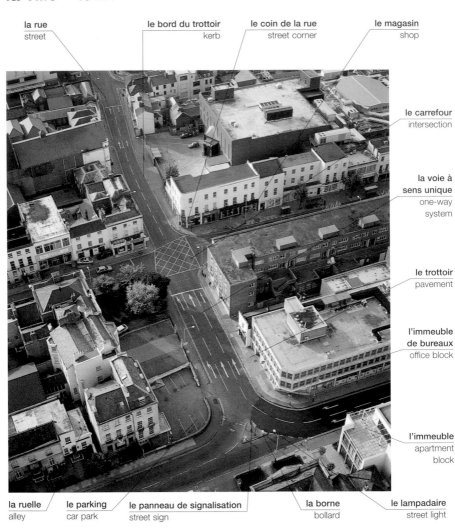

la rue
street

le bord du trottoir
kerb

le coin de la rue
street corner

le magasin
shop

le carrefour
intersection

la voie à
sens unique
one-way
system

le trottoir
pavement

l'immeuble
de bureaux
office block

l'immeuble
apartment
block

la ruelle
alley

le parking
car park

le panneau de signalisation
street sign

la borne
bollard

le lampadaire
street light

les bâtiments • buildings

la mairie
town hall

la bibliothèque
library

le cinéma
cinema

le théâtre
theatre

l'université
university

le gratte-ciel
skyscraper

les environs • areas

la zone industrielle
industrial estate

la ville
city

la banlieue
suburb

le village
village

l'école
school

---

vocabulaire • vocabulary

la zone piétonnière pedestrian zone	**la rue transversale** side street	**la bouche d'égout** manhole	**le caniveau** gutter	**l'église** church
l'avenue avenue	**la place** square	**l'arrêt de bus** bus stop	**l'usine** factory	**l'égout** drain

---

l'architecture • architecture

les bâtiments et structures • buildings and structures

le fleuron
finial

la tourelle
turret

la flèche
spire

la douve
moat

le pignon
gable

le dôme
dome

la tour
tower

la voûte
vault

la corniche
cornice

la colonne
pillar

le gratte-ciel
skyscraper

le château
castle

l'église
church

la mosquée
mosque

le temple
temple

la synagogue
synagogue

le barrage
dam

le pont
bridge

la cathédrale | cathedral

les styles • styles

gothique
gothic

l'architrave
architrave

Renaissance
Renaissance

baroque
baroque

l'arc
arch

la frise
frieze

le chœur
choir

rococo
rococo

le fronton
pediment

le contrefort
buttress

néoclassique
neoclassical

art nouveau
art nouveau

art déco
art deco

l'information
reference

l'heure • time

la grande aiguille
minute hand

la petite aiguille
hour hand

l'horloge
clock

vocabulaire • vocabulary		
la seconde second	**maintenant** now	**un quart d'heure** a quarter of an hour
la minute minute	**plus tard** later	
l'heure hour	**une demi- heure** half an hour	**vingt minutes** twenty minutes
		quarante minutes forty minutes

Quelle heure est-il?
What time is it?

Il est trois heures.
It's three o'clock.

une heure cinq
five past one

une heure dix
ten past one

une heure et quart
quarter past one

une heure vingt
twenty past one

la trotteuse
second hand

une heure vingt-cinq
twenty five past one

une heure trente
one thirty

**deux heures moins
vingt-cinq**
twenty five to two

**deux heures moins
vingt**
twenty to two

**deux heures moins
le quart**
quarter to two

deux heures moins dix
ten to two

**deux heures
moins cinq**
five to two

deux heures
two o'clock

la nuit et le jour • night and day

minuit
midnight

le lever du soleil
sunrise

l'aube
dawn

le matin
morning

le coucher du soleil
sunset

(le) midi
midday

le crépuscule
dusk

le soir
evening

l'après-midi
afternoon

vocabulaire • vocabulary

tôt early	**Tu es en avance.** You're early.	**Sois à l'heure, s'il te plaît.** Please be on time.	**Ça finit à quelle heure?** What time does it finish?
à l'heure on time	**Tu es en retard.** You're late.	**À tout à l'heure.** I'll see you later.	**Il se fait tard.** It's getting late.
tard late	**J'y arriverai bientôt.** I'll be there soon.	**Ça commence à quelle heure?** What time does it start?	**Ça dure combien de temps?** How long will it last?

le calendrier • calendar

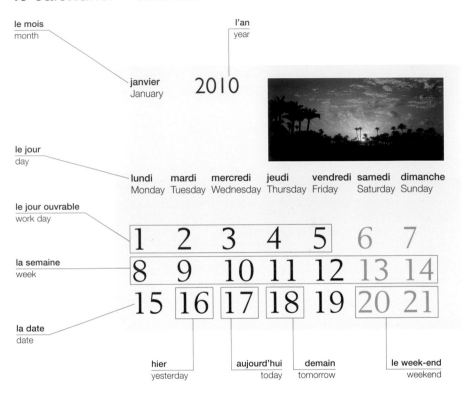

le mois
month

l'an
year

janvier
January

2010

le jour
day

lundi	**mardi**	**mercredi**	**jeudi**	**vendredi**	**samedi**	**dimanche**
Monday	Tuesday	Wednesday	Thursday	Friday	Saturday	Sunday

le jour ouvrable
work day

la semaine
week

la date
date

1	2	3	4	5	6	7
8	9	10	11	12	13	14
15	16	17	18	19	20	21

hier
yesterday

aujourd'hui
today

demain
tomorrow

le week-end
weekend

---

vocabulaire • vocabulary

janvier	**mars**	**mai**	**juillet**	**septembre**	**novembre**
January	March	May	July	September	November
février	**avril**	**juin**	**août**	**octobre**	**décembre**
February	April	June	August	October	December

---

les ans • years

1900   **mille neuf cents** • nineteen hundred

1901   **mille neuf cent un** • nineteen hundred and one

1910   **mille neuf cent dix** • nineteen ten

2000   **deux mille** • two thousand

2001   **deux mille un** • two thousand and one

les saisons • seasons

le printemps   **l'été**   **l'automne**   **l'hiver**
spring   summer   autumn   winter

vocabulaire • vocabulary

le siècle
century

la décennie
decade

le millénaire
millennium

quinze jours
fortnight

cette semaine
this week

la semaine dernière
last week

la semaine prochaine
next week

avant-hier
the day before yesterday

après-demain
the day after tomorrow

hebdomadaire
weekly

mensuel
monthly

annuel
annual

Quelle est la date aujourd'hui?
What's the date today?

C'est le sept février deux mille deux.
It's February seventh, two thousand and two.

les nombres • numbers

0	**zéro** • zero	20	**vingt** • twenty
1	**un** • one	21	**vingt et un** • twenty-one
2	**deux** • two	22	**vingt-deux** • twenty-two
3	**trois** • three	30	**trente** • thirty
4	**quatre** • four	40	**quarante** • forty
5	**cinq** • five	50	**cinquante** • fifty
6	**six** • six	60	**soixante** • sixty
7	**sept** • seven	70	**soixante-dix** • seventy
8	**huit** • eight	80	**quatre-vingts** • eighty
9	**neuf** • nine	90	**quatre-vingt-dix** • ninety
10	**dix** • ten	100	**cent** • one hundred
11	**onze** • eleven	110	**cent dix** • one hundred and ten
12	**douze** • twelve	200	**deux cents** • two hundred
13	**treize** • thirteen	300	**trois cents** • three hundred
14	**quatorze** • fourteen	400	**quatre cents** • four hundred
15	**quinze** • fifteen	500	**cinq cents** • five hundred
16	**seize** • sixteen	600	**six cents** • six hundred
17	**dix-sept** • seventeen	700	**sept cents** • seven hundred
18	**dix-huit** • eighteen	800	**huit cents** • eight hundred
19	**dix-neuf** • nineteen	900	**neuf cents** • nine hundred

1000	**mille** • one thousand	
10,000	**dix mille** • ten thousand	
20,000	**vingt mille** • twenty thousand	
50,000	**cinquante mille** • fifty thousand	
55,500	**cinqante-cinq mille cinq cents** • fifty-five thousand five hundred	
100,000	**cent mille** • one hundred thousand	
1,000,000	**un million** • one million	
1,000,000,000	**un milliard** • one billion	

premier
first

deuxième
second

troisième
third

quatrième • fourth

cinquième • fifth

sixième • sixth

septième • seventh

huitième • eighth

neuvième • ninth

dixième • tenth

onzième • eleventh

douzième • twelfth

treizième • thirteenth

quatorzième • fourteenth

quinzième • fifteenth

seizième
• sixteenth

dix-septième
• seventeenth

dix-huitième
• eighteenth

dix-neuvième
• nineteenth

vingtième •
twentieth

vingt et unième
• twenty-first

vingt-deuxième
• twenty-second

vingt-troisième
• twenty-third

trentième • thirtieth

quarantième • fortieth

cinquantième • fiftieth

soixantième • sixtieth

soixante-dixième
• seventieth

quatre-vingtième
• eightieth

quatre-vingt-dixième
• ninetieth

centième
• one hundredth

les poids et mesures • weights and measures

la superficie • area

le pied carré	**le mètre carré**
square foot	square metre

la distance • distance

le kilomètre	**le mile**
kilometre	mile

le plateau
pan

la livre
pound

l'once
ounce

le kilogramme
kilogram

le gramme
gram

KRUPS

la balance | scales

---

vocabulaire • vocabulary

le yard	**la tonne**	**mesurer**
yard	tonne	measure (v)
le mètre	**le milligramme**	**peser**
metre	milligram	weigh (v)

---

la longueur • length

le pied
foot

le millimètre	**le centimètre**	**le pouce**
millimetre	centimetre	inch

---

la capacité • capacity

le demi-litre
half-litre

la pinte
pint

le volume
volume

le millilitre
millilitre

le verre mesureur
measuring jug

la mesure pour les liquides
liquid measure

le récipient • container

le sac
bag

la brique
carton

le paquet
packet

la bouteille
bottle

la boîte
can

le pot | tub

le pot | jar

la boîte | tin

le pulvérisateur
liquid dispenser

le pain
bar

le tube
tube

le rouleau
roll

le paquet
pack

la bombe
spray can

français • english

311

la carte du monde • world map

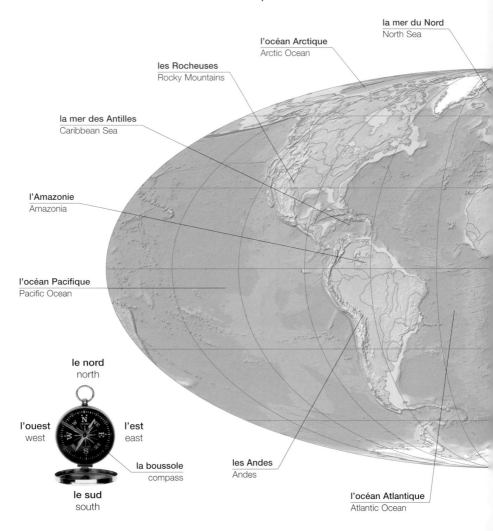

la mer du Nord
North Sea

l'océan Arctique
Arctic Ocean

les Rocheuses
Rocky Mountains

la mer des Antilles
Caribbean Sea

l'Amazonie
Amazonia

l'océan Pacifique
Pacific Ocean

le nord
north

l'ouest
west

l'est
east

la boussole
compass

les Andes
Andes

le sud
south

l'océan Atlantique
Atlantic Ocean

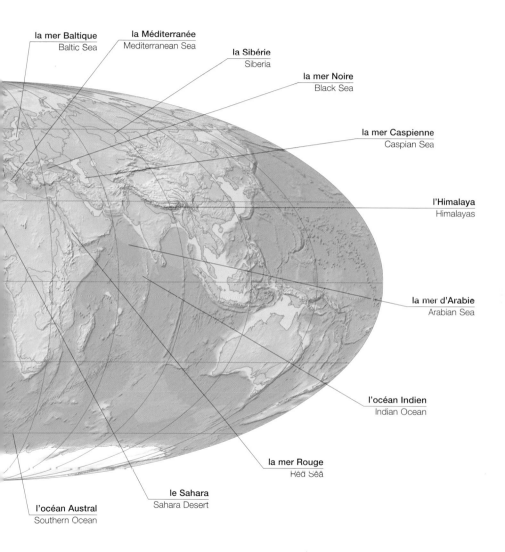

la mer Baltique
Baltic Sea

la Méditerranée
Mediterranean Sea

la Sibérie
Siberia

la mer Noire
Black Sea

la mer Caspienne
Caspian Sea

l'Himalaya
Himalayas

la mer d'Arabie
Arabian Sea

l'océan Indien
Indian Ocean

la mer Rouge
Red Sea

le Sahara
Sahara Desert

l'océan Austral
Southern Ocean

l'Amérique du Nord et centrale • North and Central America

1 **l'Alaska** • Alaska
2 **le Canada** • Canada
3 **le Groenland** • Greenland
4 **les États-Unis d'Amérique** • United States of America
5 **le Mexique** • Mexico
6 **le Guatemala** • Guatemala
7 **(le) Bélize** • Belize
8 **Le Salvador** • El Salvador
9 **le Honduras** • Honduras
10 **le Nicaragua** • Nicaragua
11 **le Costa Rica** • Costa Rica
12 **le Panama** • Panama
13 **Cuba** • Cuba
14 **les Bahamas** • Bahamas
15 **la Jamaïque** • Jamaica
16 **Haïti** • Haiti
17 **la République dominicaine** • Dominican Republic
18 **la Porto Rico** • Puerto Rico
19 **la Barbade** • Barbados
20 **la Trinité-et-Tobago** • Trinidad and Tobago
21 **Saint-Kitts-et-Nevis** • St. Kitts and Nevis

22 **Antigua-et-Barbuda** • Antigua and Barbuda
23 **la Dominique** • Dominica
24 **Sainte-Lucie** • St Lucia
25 **Saint-Vincent-et-les-Grenadines** • St Vincent and The Grenadines
26 **la Grenade** • Grenada

l'Amérique du Sud • South America

1 **le Venezuela** • Venezuela

2 **la Colombie** • Colombia

3 **l'Équateur** • Ecuador

4 **le Pérou** • Peru

5 **les îles Galapagos**
• Galapagos Islands

6 **la Guyane** • Guyana

7 **le Surinam** • Suriname

8 **la Guyane française**
• French Guiana

9 **le Brésil** • Brazil

10 **la Bolivie** • Bolivia

11 **le Chili** • Chile

12 **l'Argentine** • Argentina

13 **le Paraguay** • Paraguay

14 **l'Uruguay** • Uruguay

15 **les îles Malouines**
• Falkland Islands

vocabulaire • vocabulary		
le pays country	**la province** province	**la zone** zone
la nation nation	**le territoire** territory	**le district** district
l'État state	**la colonie** colony	**la région** region
le continent continent	**la principauté** principality	**la capitale** capital

français • english

l'Europe • Europe

1 l'Irlande • Ireland
2 le Royaume-Uni • United Kingdom
3 le Portugal • Portugal
4 l'Espagne • Spain
5 les Baléares • Balearic Islands
6 l'Andorre • Andorra
7 la France • France
8 la Belgique • Belgium
9 les Pays-Bas • Netherlands
10 le Luxembourg • Luxembourg
11 l'Allemagne • Germany
12 le Danemark • Denmark
13 la Norvège • Norway
14 la Suède • Sweden
15 la Finlande • Finland
16 l'Estonie • Estonia
17 la Lettonie • Latvia
18 la Lituanie • Lithuania
19 Kaliningrad • Kaliningrad
20 la Pologne • Poland
21 la République tchèque • Czech Republic
22 l'Autriche • Austria
23 le Liechtenstein • Liechtenstein
24 la Suisse • Switzerland
25 l'Italie • Italy
26 Monaco • Monaco
27 la Corse • Corsica
28 la Sardaigne • Sardinia

29 le Saint-Marin • San Marino
30 la Cité du Vatican • Vatican City
31 la Sicile • Sicily
32 Malte • Malta
33 la Slovénie • Slovenia
34 la Croatie • Croatia
35 la Hongrie • Hungary
36 la Slovaquie • Slovakia
37 l'Ukraine • Ukraine
38 la Bélarus • Belarus

39 la Moldavie • Moldova
40 la Roumanie • Romania
41 la Yougoslavie • Yugoslavia
42 la Bosnie-Herzégovine • Bosnia and Herzogovina
43 l'Albanie • Albania
44 la Macédonie • Macedonia
45 la Bulgarie • Bulgaria
46 la Grèce • Greece
47 la Turquie • Turkey
48 Chypre • Cyprus

l'Afrique • Africa

1 **le Maroc** • Morocco

2 **le Sahara occidental**
 • Western Sahara

3 **la Mauritanie**
 • Mauritania

4 **le Sénégal** • Senegal

5 **la Gambie** • Gambia

6 **la Guinée-Bissau**
 • Guinea-Bissau

7 **la Guinée** • Guinea

8 **la Sierra Leone**
 • Sierra Leone

9 **le Libéria** • Liberia

10 **la Côte d'Ivoire**
 • Ivory Coast

11 **le Burkina** • Burkina Faso

12 **le Mali** • Mali

13 **l'Algérie** • Algeria

14 **la Tunisie** • Tunisia

15 **la Libye** • Libya

16 **le Niger** • Niger

17 **le Ghana** • Ghana

18 **le Togo** • Togo

19 **le Bénin** • Benin

20 **le Nigéria** • Nigeria

21 **Sao Tomé-et-Principe**
 • São Tomé and Principe

22 **la Guinée équatoriale**
 • Equatorial Guinea

23 **le Cameroun** • Cameroon

24 **le Tchad** • Chad

25 **l'Égypte** • Egypt

26 **le Soudan** • Sudan

27 **l'Érythrée** • Eritrea

28 **Djibouti** • Djibouti

29 **l'Éthiopie** • Ethiopia

30 **la Somalie** • Somalia

31 **le Kenya** • Kenya

32 **l'Ouganda** • Uganda

33 **la République centrafricaine**
 • Central African Republic

34 **le Gabon** • Gabon

35 **le Congo** • Congo

36 **Cabinda** • Cabinda

37 **la République démocratique du Congo** • Democratic Republic of the Congo

38 **le Rwanda** • Rwanda

39 **le Burundi** • Burundi

40 **la Tanzanie** • Tanzania

41 **le Mozambique**
 • Mozambique

42 **le Malawi** • Malawi

43 **la Zambie** • Zambia

44 **l'Angola** • Angola

45 **la Namibie** • Namibia

46 **le Botswana** • Botswana

47 **le Zimbabwe** • Zimbabwe

48 **l'Afrique du Sud**
 • South Africa

49 **le Lesotho** • Lesotho

50 **le Swaziland** • Swaziland

51 **les Comores** • Comoros

52 **Madagascar** • Madagascar

53 **l'île Maurice** • Mauritius

l'Asie • Asia

1 **la Fédération de Russie**
   • Russian Federation

2 **la Géorgie** • Georgia

3 **l'Arménie** • Armenia

4 **l'Azerbaïdjan** • Azerbaijan

5 **l'Iran** • Iran

6 **l'Irak** • Iraq

7 **la Syrie** • Syria

8 **le Liban** • Lebanon

9 **Israël** • Israel

10 **la Jordanie** • Jordan

11 **l'Arabie Saoudite**
   • Saudi Arabia

12 **le Koweït** • Kuwait

13 **le Qatar** • Qatar

14 **les Émirats arabes unis**
   • United Arab Emirates

15 **l'Oman** • Oman

16 **le Yémen** • Yemen

17 **le Kasakhastan** • Kazakhstan

18 **l'Ouzbékistan** • Uzbekistan

19 **le Turkmenistan** • Turkmenistan

20 **l'Afghanistan** • Afghanistan

21 **le Tadjikistan** • Tajikistan

22 **le Kirghizistan** • Kyrgyzstan

23 **le Pakistan** • Pakistan

24 **l'Inde** • India

25 **les Maldives** • Maldives

26 **Sri Lanka** • Sri Lanka

27 **la Chine** • China

28 **la Mongolie** • Mongolia

29 **la Corée du Nord** • North Korea

30 **la Corée du Sud** • South Korea

31 **le Japon** • Japan

32 **le Népal** • Nepal

33 **le Bhoutan** • Bhutan

34 **le Bangladesh** • Bangladesh

35 **la Birmanie
   (le Myanmar)**
   • Burma (Myanmar)

36 **la Thaïlande** • Thailand

37 **le Laos** • Laos

38 **le Vietnam** • Viet Nam

39 **le Cambodge** • Cambodia

40 **la Malaisie** • Malaysia

l'**Australasie** • Australasia

1 **l'Australie** • Australia
2 **la Tasmanie** • Tasmania
3 **la Nouvelle-Zélande** • New Zealand

41 **Singapour** • Singapore
42 **l'Indonésie** • Indonesia
43 **le Brunei** • Brunei
44 **les Philippines** • Philippines
45 **Taiwan** • **Taiwan**
46 **le Timor oriental** • East Timor
47 **la Papouasie-Nouvelle-Guinée**
   • Papua New Guinea
48 **les îles Salomon** • Solomon Islands
49 **Vanuatu** • Vanuatu

particules et antonymes • particles and antonyms

à to	**de** from	**pour** for	**vers** towards
au-dessus de over	**sous** under	**le long de** along	**à travers** across
devant in front of	**derrière** behind	**avec** with	**sans** without
sur onto	**dans** into	**avant** before	**après** after
dans in	**dehors** out	**avant** by	**jusqu'à** until
au-dessus de above	**au-dessous de** below	**tôt** early	**tard** late
à l'intérieur de inside	**à l'extérieur de** outside	**maintenant** now	**plus tard** later
en haut up	**en bas** down	**toujours** always	**jamais** never
à at	**au-delà de** beyond	**souvent** often	**rarement** rarely
à travers through	**autour de** around	**hier** yesterday	**demain** tomorrow
sur on top of	**à côté de** beside	**premier** first	**dernier** last
entre between	**en face de** opposite	**chaque** every	**quelque** some
près de near	**loin de** far	**vers** about	**exactement** exactly
ici here	**là** there	**un peu** a little	**beaucoup** a lot

grand large	**petit** small	**chaud** hot	**froid** cold
large wide	**étroit** narrow	**ouvert** open	**fermé** closed
grand tall	**court** short	**plein** full	**vide** empty
haut high	**bas** low	**neuf** new	**vieux** old
épais thick	**mince** thin	**clair** light	**foncé** dark
léger light	**lourd** heavy	**facile** easy	**difficile** difficult
dur hard	**mou** soft	**libre** free	**occupé** occupied
humide wet	**sec** dry	**fort** strong	**faible** weak
bon good	**mauvais** bad	**gros** fat	**mince** thin
rapide fast	**lent** slow	**jeune** young	**vieux** old
juste correct	**faux** wrong	**mieux** better	**pire** worse
propre clean	**sale** dirty	**noir** black	**blanc** white
beau beautiful	**laid** ugly	**intéressant** interesting	**ennuyeux** boring
cher expensive	**bon marché** cheap	**malade** sick	**bien** well
silencieux quiet	**bruyant** noisy	**le début** beginning	**la fin** end

phrases utiles • useful phrases

phrases essentielles
• essential phrases

Oui
Yes

Non
No

Peut-être
Maybe

S'il vous plaît
Please

Merci
Thank you

De rien
You're welcome

Pardon
Excuse me

Je suis désolé
I'm sorry

Ne... pas
Don't

D'accord
OK

Très bien
That's fine

C'est juste
That's correct

C'est faux
That's wrong

salutations
• greetings

Bonjour
Hello

Au revoir
Goodbye

Bonjour
Good morning

Bonjour
Good afternoon

Bonsoir
Good evening

Bonne nuit
Good night

Comment allez-vous?
How are you?

Je m'appelle...
My name is...

Vous vous appelez comment?
What is your name?

Il/Elle s'appelle comment?
What is his/her name?

Je vous présente...
May I introduce...

C'est...
This is...

Enchanté
Pleased to meet you

À tout à l'heure
See you later

panneaux • signs

Office de tourisme
Tourist information

Entrée
Entrance

Sortie
Exit

Sortie de secours
Emergency exit

Poussez
Push

Danger
Danger

Défense de fumer
No smoking

En panne
Out of order

Heures d'ouverture
Opening times

Entrée gratuite
Free admission

Journée continue
Open all day

Prix réduit
Reduced price

Soldes
Sale

Frappez avant d'entrer
Knock before entering

Défense de marcher sur la pelouse
Keep off the grass

assistance • help

Pouvez-vous m'aider?
Can you help me?

Je ne comprends pas
I don't understand

Je ne sais pas
I don't know

Vous parlez anglais, français...?
Do you speak English, French...?

Je parle anglais, espagnol...
I speak English, Spanish...

Parlez moins vite, s'il vous plaît
Please speak more slowly

Écrivez-le pour moi, s'il vous plaît
Please write it down for me

J'ai perdu...
I have lost...

directions
• directions

Je me suis perdu
I am lost

Où est le/la...?
Where is the...?

Où est le/la...le/la plus proche?
Where is the nearest...?

Où sont les toilettes?
Where are the toilets?

Pour aller à...?
How do I get to...?

À droite
To the right

À gauche
To the left

Tout droit
Straight ahead

C'est loin...?
How far is...?

les panneaux routiers
• road signs

Toutes directions
All directions

Prudence
Caution

Entrée interdite
No entry

Ralentir
Slow down

Déviation
Diversion

Serrez à droite
Keep to the right

Autoroute
Motorway

Stationnement interdit
No parking

Passage interdit
No through road

Sens unique
One-way street

Autres directions
Other directions

Riverains autorisés
Residents only

Travaux
Roadworks

Virage dangereux
Dangerous bend

logement •
accommodation

J'ai réservé une chambre
I have a reservation

Où est la salle à manger?
Where is the dining room?

Le numéro de ma chambre est le ...
My room number is ...

Le petit déjeuner est à quelle heure?
What time is breakfast?

Je serai de retour à ... heures
I'll be back at ... o'clock

Je pars demain
I'm leaving tomorrow

nourriture et boissons
• eating and drinking

À la vôtre!
Cheers!

C'est délicieux/terrible
It's delicious/awful

Je ne bois/fume pas
I don't drink/smoke

Je ne mange pas de la viande
I don't eat meat

Je n'en veux plus, merci
No more for me, thank you

Encore un peu, s'il vous plaît.
May I have some more?

L'addition, s'il vous plaît.
May we have the bill?

Je voudrais un reçu.
Can I have a receipt?

Partie non-fumeurs
No-smoking area

la santé
• health

Je ne me sens pas bien
I don't feel well

J'ai envie de vomir
I feel sick

Pouvez-vous me donner le numéro de téléphone du docteur le plus proche?
What is the telephone number of the nearest doctor?

J'ai mal ici
It hurts here

J'ai de la fièvre
I have a temperature

Je suis enceinte de ...mois
I'm ... months pregnant

J'ai besoin d'une ordonnance pour ...
I need a prescription for ...

Je prends habituellement ...
I normally take ...

Je suis allergique à ...
I'm allergic to ...

index français • French index

français

français

français

français

français

français

français

français

français

français

français

français

français

français • english

français

index anglais • English index

english

english

english

english

english

english

english

english

english

english

english

english

english

english

english

english

remerciements • acknowledgments

DORLING KINDERSLEY would like to thank Tracey Miles and Christine Lacey for design assistance, Georgina Garner for editorial and administrative help, Sonia Gavira, Polly Boyd, and Cathy Meeus for editorial help, and Claire Bowers for compiling the DK picture credits.

The publisher would like to thank the following for their kind permission to reproduce their photographs:
Abbreviations key:
t = top, b = bottom, r = right, l = left, c = centre

Abode: 62; **Action Plus:** 224bc; **alamy.com:** 154t; A.T. Willett 287bcl; Michael Foyle 184bl; Stock Connection 287bcr; **Allsport/Getty Images:** 238cl; **Alvey and Towers:** 209 acr, 215bcl, 215bcr, 241cr; **Peter Anderson:** 188cbr, 271br. **Anthony Blake Photo Library:** Charlie Stebbings 114cl; John Sims 114tcl; **Andyalte:** 98tl; **apple mac computers:** 268tcr; **Arcaid:** John Edward Linden 301bl; Martine Hamilton Knight, Architects: Chapman Taylor Partners, 213cl; Richard Bryant 301br; **Argos:** 41tcl, 66cbl, 66cl, 66br, 66bcl, 69cl, 70bcl, 71t, 77tl, 269tc, 270tl; **Axiom:** Eitan Simanor 105bcr; Ian Cumming 104; Vicki Couchman 148cr; **Beken Of Cowes Ltd:** 215cbc; **Bosch:** 76tcr, 76tc, 76tcl; **Camera Press:** 27c, 38tr, 256t, 257cr; Barry J. Holmes 148tr; Jane Hanger 159cr; Mary Germanou 259bc; **Corbis:** 78b; Anna Clopet 247tr; Bettmann 181tl, 181tr; Bo Zauders 156t; Bob Rowan 152bl; Bob Winsett 247cbl; Brian Bailey 247br; Carl and Ann Purcell 162l; Chris Rainer 247ctl; ChromoSohm Inc. 179cr; Craig Aurness 215bl; David H.Wells 249cbr; Dennis Marsico 274bl; Dimitri Lundt 236bc; Duomo 211tl; Gail Mooney 277ctcr; George Lepp 248c; Gunter Marx 248cr; Jack Fields 210b; Jack Hollingsworth 231bl; Jacqui Hurst 277cbr; James L. Amos 247bl, 191ctr, 220bcr; Jan Butchofsky 277cbc; Johnathan Blair 243cr; Jon Feingersh 153tr; Jose F. Poblete 191br; Jose Luis Pelaez.Inc 153tc, 175tl; Karl Weatherly 220bl, 247tcr; Kelly Mooney Photography 259tl; Kevin Fleming 249bc; Kevin R. Morris 105tr, 243tl, 243tc; Kim Sayer 249tcr; Lynn Goldsmith 258t; Macduff Everton 231bcl; Mark Gibson 249bl; Mark L. Stephenson 249tcl; Michael Pole 115tr; Michael S. Yamashita 247ctcl; Mike King 247cbl; Neil Rabinowitz 214br; Owen Franken 112t; Pablo Corral 115bc; Paul A.

Sounders 169br, 249ctcl; Paul J. Sutton 224c, 224br; Peter Turnley 105tcr; Phil Schermeister 227b, 248tr; R. W Jones 309; R.W. Jones 175tr; Richard Hutchings 168b; Rick Doyle 241ctr; Robert Holmes 97br, 277ctc; Roger Ressmeyer 169tr; Russ Schleipman 229; Steve Raymer 168cr; The Purcell Team 211ctr; Tim Wright 178; Vince Streano 194t; Wally McNamee 220br, 220bcl, 224bl; Yann Arhus-Bertrand 249tl; **Demetrio Carrasco / Dorling Kindersley (c) Herge / Les Editions Casterman:** 112ccl; **Dixons:** 270cl, 270cr, 270bl, 270bcl, 270bcr, 270ccr; **Education Photos:** John Walmsley 26tl; **Empics Ltd:** Adam Day 236br; Andy Heading 243c; Steve White 249cbc; **Getty Images:** 48bcl, 100t, 114bcr, 154bl, 287tr; 94tr; **Dennis Gilbert:** 106tc; **Hulsta:** 70t; **Ideal Standard Ltd:** 72r; **The Image Bank/Getty Images:** 58; **Impact Photos:** Eliza Armstrong 115cr; John Arthur 190tl; Philip Achache 246t; **The Interior Archive:** Henry Wilson, Alfie's Market 114bl; Luke White, Architect: David Mikhail, 59tl; Simon Upton, Architect: Phillippe Starck, St Martins Lane Hotel 100bcr, 100br; **Jason Hawkes Aerial Photography:** 216t; **Dan Johnson:** 26cbl, 35r; **Kos Pictures Source:** 215cbl, 240tc, 240tr; David Williams 216b; **Lebrecht Collection:** Kate Mount 169bc; **MP Visual.com:** Mark Swallow 202t; **NASA:** 280cr, 280ccl, 281tl; **P&O Princess Cruises:** 214bl; **P A Photos:** 181br; **The Photographers' Library:** 186bl, 186bc, 186t; **Plain and Simple Kitchens:** 66t; **Powerstock Photolibrary:** 169tl, 256t, 287tc; **Rail Images:** 208c, 208 cbl, 209br; **Red Consultancy:** Odeon cinemas 257br; **Redferns:** 259br; Nigel Crane 259c; **Rex Features:** 106br, 259tc, 259tr, 259bl, 280b; Charles Ommaney 114tcr; J.F.F Whitehead 243cl; Patrick Barth 101tl; Patrick Frilet 189cbl; Scott Wiseman 287bl; **Royalty Free Images:** Getty Images/Eyewire 154bl; **Science & Society Picture Library:** Science Museum 202b; **Skyscan:** 168t, 182c, 298; Quick UK Ltd 212; **Sony:** 268bc; **Robert Streeter:** 154br; **Neil Sutherland:** 82tr, 83tl, 90t, 118, 188ctr, 196tl, 196tr, 299cl, 299bl; **The Travel Library:** Stuart Black 264t; **Travelex:** 97cl; **Vauxhall:** Technik 198t, 199tl, 199tr, 199cl, 199cr, 199cctcl, 199ctcr, 199tcl, 199tcr, 200; **View Pictures:** Dennis Gilbert, Architects: ACDP Consulting, 106t; Dennis Gilbert,

Chris Wilkinson Architects, 209tr; Peter Cook, Architects: Nicholas Crimshaw and partners, 208t; **Betty Walton:** 185br; **Colin Walton:** 2, 4, 7, 9, 10, 28, 42, 56, 92, 95c, 99tl, 99tcl, 102, 116, 120t, 138t, 146, 150t, 160, 170, 191ctcl, 192, 218, 252, 260br, 260l, 261tr, 261c, 261cr, 271cbl, 271cbr, 271ctl, 278, 287br, 302, 401.

DK PICTURE LIBRARY:
Akhil Bahkshi; Patrick Baldwin; Geoff Brightling; British Museum; John Bulmer; Andrew Butler; Joe Cornish; Brian Cosgrove; Andy Crawford and Kit Hougton; Philip Dowell; Alistair Duncan; Gables; Bob Gathany; Norman Hollands; Kew Gardens; Peter James Kindersley; Vladimir Kozlik; Sam Lloyd; London Northern Bus Company Ltd; Tracy Morgan; David Murray and Jules Selmes; Musée Vivant du Cheval, France; Museum of Broadcast Communications; Museum of Natural History; NASA; National History Museum; Norfolk Rural Life Museum; Stephen Oliver; RNLI; Royal Ballet School; Guy Ryecart; Science Museum; Neil Setchfield; Ross Simms and the Winchcombe Folk Police Museum; Singapore Symphony Orchestra; Smart Museum of Art; Tony Souter; Erik Svensson and Jeppe Wikstrom; Sam Tree of Keygrove Marketing Ltd; Barrie Watts; Alan Williams; Jerry Young.

Additional Photography by Colin Walton.

Colin Walton would like to thank:
A&A News, Uckfield; Abbey Music, Tunbridge Wells; Arena Mens Clothing, Tunbridge Wells; Burrells of Tunbridge Wells; Gary at Di Marco's; Jeremy's Home Store, Tunbridge Wells; Noakes of Tunbridge Wells; Ottakar's, Tunbridge Wells; Selby's of Uckfield; Sevenoaks Sound and Vision; Westfield, Royal Victoria Place, Tunbridge Wells.

All other images are Dorling Kindersley copyright. For further information see www.dkimages.com